·F·L·O·W·E·R·
ARRANGING

JANICE HARPER

GALLERY BOOKS
An imprint of W.H. Smith Publishers Inc.
112 Madison Avenue
New York, New York 10016

For George and Andrew

A QUINTET BOOK
produced for
GALLERY BOOKS
An imprint of W.H. Smith Publishers Inc.
112 Madison Avenue
New York, New York 10016

ISBN 0-8317-0063-7

This book was designed and produced by
Quintet Publishing Limited
6 Blundell Street
London N7 9BH

Art Director: Peter Bridgewater
Designer: Ian Hunt
Editors: Patricia Bayer, Louise Bostock
Photographer: Ian Howes
Illustrator: Lorraine Harrison

Typeset in Great Britain by
Central Southern Typesetters, Eastbourne
Manufactured in Hong Kong by Regent
Publishing Services Limited
Printed in Hong Kong by
Leefung-Asco Printers Limited

CONTENTS

Introduction   6

PART I

Equipment, Techniques and Basic Principles   9

The Mechanics and Equipment Needed   10

Floral and Foliate Plant Material   17

Aesthetics and Advice for Advanced Flower
Arrangers   28

PART II

The Flower Arrangements   37

Conclusion   108

Bibliography   109

Index   110

Acknowledgements   112

Introduction

*F*lower arrangers have always been telling me that they would like a practical book on flower arranging, with an emphasis on economical use of flowers, and over the years I have been gathering hints and tips that will help give them – and you – more enjoyment from flowers.

Economical designs are featured in this book, as well as modern arrangements that make the most of a few flowers. For those of you who are advanced arrangers, I have included ways in which you can further your studies.

I love everything that grows, and as flower lovers and arrangers I am sure you do, too, from the showiest blossoms down to the humblest foliage, all of which can give us so much enjoyment. It is the art of placing the right materials together that makes a design, and, whether you use exotic blooms or wild flowers, as long as your plant material is chosen with care you can create a pleasing and handsome arrangement.

More than anything, it is important for you, the flower arranger, to keep an open mind, and to open your eyes to the wonderful things that nature produces.

PART ONE

EQUIPMENT
TECHNIQUES AND
BASIC PRINCIPLES

Students of flower arranging, and housewives who wish to have flowers about the house without paying a fortune for them, are the persons for whom this book is primarily intended. It is relatively easy to make attractive flower arrangements without spending too much money — if you know some of the tricks of the trade.

You will need certain staple items in order to make your flower arranging an enjoyable task, but once you purchase them, you can then rely on what is readily on hand to create flower arrangements for your home.

LEFT *This curved arrangement forms a canopy over a delicate figurine.*

The Mechanics and Equipment Needed

BASIC INFORMATION

You will need a good heavy pinholder, a pair of flower scissors or pruners, about 1½ft (45cm) of 2–2½in (5–6.3cm) wire mesh, a block of water-retaining floral foam and a small amount of adhesive clay for anchoring arrangements (available in rolls as Oasis-Fix). Florists and garden centres sell foam and pinholders, and wire mesh can be bought at hardware shops.

A 3in (7.6cm) pinholder is a good-sized one for a beginner, as it is heavy enough to support a substantial arrangement. You should stick it down with three small pills of adhesive clay or modelling clay, but make sure the surfaces are dry. You should have the selvages removed from the wire mesh so that its long cut edges can then help you control your flowers by twisting them around the stems. The pinholder is best in low containers, used by itself for modern arrangements or in conjunction with wire mesh if you intend to make an arrangement with many flowers. This method requires pressing the stretched-out wire between the pins on the holder, then gently folding in the remainder to fit your container (you will need to adjust the amount of wire needed for each individual container). It can be held in place with rubber bands over the container and the wire.

The floral foam is useful in stemmed containers so that the flowers can flow over the sides easily. At least ½in (1.3cm) should come above the rim of the container. It is also very useful when you wish to give flowers as a gift, since it is quite portable. You can also use it with the pinholder or wire mesh.

You can rely on small pebbles for emergency mechanics. They will not allow you to make a controlled design, but at least they can lend a bit of support to the flowers. Criss-crossing adhesive tape is another emergency form of mechanics, only suitable for small lightweight arrangements (again, it does not give you a great deal of control over your arrangement). The advanced flower arranger would be advised to have pinholders in various sizes to meet different needs for the various designs.

STANDARD CONTAINERS

You will notice that up until now I have not mentioned the word 'vase'. That's because to a flower arranger any container that is capable of holding water or floral foam can be pressed into use. There is no need to rush out and buy expensive containers, since there are many things about the house that you can use – jugs, coffee mugs, baking dishes, ashtrays, even that old teapot with a broken lid. I'm sure that if you have a good rummage round you will find any number of things you can put into service.

You should purchase a little device called a candle cup, preferably one made of metal – it can be inserted into the top of candlesticks and bottles to give you a raised container. Wind a little piece of adhesive clay sausage-like around the rim of the candlestick or bottle and push the nozzle into the hole. Tape the cup to the bottle for extra holding power. The reason for recommending a metal one is that metal sticks much better to glass and china than plastic does, although the plastic variety is fine for wooden items.

If you want to add to your collection of containers without spending too much money, go to charity (thrift) shops, jumble (rummage) sales, car boot sales, swap meets, flea markets and junk shops, where you may well be able to find something that you can use, if not an outright treasure. Just make sure that it has a good shape and is *in* good shape – you can always give the receptacle a coat of paint if you don't like the colour.

One of my favourite containers came from a summer fair. It was in the most hideous shade of green you could imagine, and would have clashed wildly with any foliage used in it. But still I took it home, where I found a few old tin cans of paint in the shed with a scant scraping of useable paint at the bottom. I had just enough dark brown to paint the container completely. Then I trickled a very small amount of beige paint on top of the brown, brushing it in with a light downward stroke. I was most pleased with the result, which gave the vessel an interesting pottery glaze. I'm telling you this story to remind you that flower arrangers seldom throw anything away!

MAKING YOUR OWN CONTAINERS

A good way of saving money – and unleashing your creativity – is to have a go at making your own containers. The basic ingredients for doing this are yoghurt cartons, empty tin cans, fabrics, leftover pieces of braid, stick-on plastic, bleach and liquid detergent bottles, paint, glue and other finishing materials.

The easiest container is a simple bleach bottle – cut off the nozzle end, level off the top and paint it. Or, if straight-sided, cover it with glued-on fabric. Cut the fabric about 1in (25cm) larger than the perimeter of the container and glue under ¼in (.6cm) on one long side so that this can be stuck on top of the other long side. Finish off the top and bottom with a length of braid.

Bind string around a tin can to give it an interesting texture; you only need to glue the ends. Cover a bleach bottle (one of the smooth straight ones) with a piece of

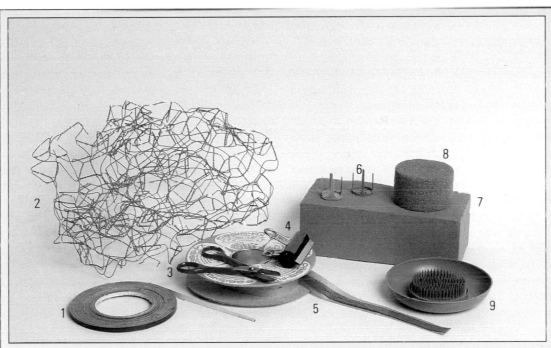

Basic Equipment

ABOVE *(left to right)* 1 *Floral tape.* 2 *Wire mesh.* 3 *Mini-secateurs.* 4 *Bulldog clip.* 5 *Oasis-fix.* 6 *Oasis pin.* 7 *Large block of green foam.* 8 *Dry foam for dried and fabric arrangements.* 9 *Small oasis bowl.*

Special Equipment

ABOVE *(left to right)* 1 *Water-resistant satin ribbon.* 2 *Polypropylene ribbon.* 3 *Combined pinholder and small container.* 4 *Candle-cups.* 5 *Gold spray.* 6 *Coloured spray.* 7 *Clearlife – to prolong the vase life of some fresh flowers.* 8 *Kerishine – for imparting a shine to foliage.* 9 *Floral tape.* 10 *Stub wires.* 11 *Silver binding wires.*

contact paper or other adhesive-backed plastic material. It will take you all of five minutes to do. For these containers the width used for covering shelves is sufficient. You can also make a quick base to match. If it is round or oval, snip the plastic to the rim at about ½in (1.3cm) intervals before pressing down to the underside; this will give a neat finish to the base.

With tall containers that you have made, the simplest form of mechanics is leftover floral foam three-quarters of the way up, and a new piece in the remainder. However, should you wish to use a small pinholder, you will need a small tin can that fits snugly into the top of the container; then fill the container with made-up filler compound to the bottom of the tin can, making sure that the can is level with the rim of the container. Allow the filler to dry out before putting the tin into the final position. Small plastic containers such as those used for ice cream or cream can be stuck together with a strong glue. Stick them together at their bases (one being upside-down), and when the glue has dried paint in the colour of your choice. If you want, finish off with narrow Russian braid at the top and bottom.

Cans such as the flattish ones that you get pineapple slices in can have split bamboo cut to size and stuck all around its sides.

Try different textures for covering cans and bottles. For instance, lightly apply filler compound over the surface, then rough it up or make a pattern on it with a fork. Or, cover the container with glue and roll it in sand and sawdust. Some of the results may be a bit fragile, but at least they will give you a variety of containers to play with.

A medium-sized roasting pan can be painted black on the outside and blue-green on the inside, which is quite attractive to use for water scenes. There are a number of cheap plastic containers on the market, and it is often worth buying these to repaint in the shade of your choice, or you could add decorative mouldings before painting to give a container a distinctive period look.

An urn with grooves can be painted in moss green, its grooves lightly touched up with black paint to give it an antique look. Or you can add a tin can the same size as the base of the container, which you can then cover with a remnant of matching velvet and finish with narrow braid. It will add both height and elegance to an inexpensive container.

It is also possible to buy screw-on bowls, which you can adapt to a table lamp by simply removing the light fittings and screwing in the bowl. Those with figurines, marble or mock onyx look attractive.

Shells are another good form of container, and even the smaller ones are fine for dainty arrangements. With most shells a piece of floral foam cut to fit will hold your plant material.

Containers can be made of wood providing you are handy with a saw. However, with wooden containers it is important to remember that they will need a lining of some sort to enable them to hold water.

I have only mentioned the very simple containers that anyone can make, but those of you who enjoy making things can experiment with your own ideas. Those of you adept at basketry and pottery can make up your own designs by drawing rough ideas before you begin.

BELOW *Glass, porcelain and plastic containers can all be used effectively.*

A wide range of vases, in different shapes, sizes and colours, will help to bring variety and interest to your designs.

CHOOSING CONTAINERS AND ACCESSORIES

At some stage in your flower-arranging career you will of course want to acquire more containers than those you have made or adapted from items about the house.

If you are buying an expensive container, first make sure that you like it, for you will have to live with it; and be sure the colour is something that will blend with plant material. My own choices would be moss or leaf green, brown or grey. Although white and black are neutral, black doesn't show soft colours to advantage, and unless all-white flowers are to be used, white containers can dominate the flowers.

As to style, it is a good idea to collect different sorts of designs. An open container with a good area inside for water scenes is useful, as is a modern container, perhaps one with two openings that can increase the ways you can use it. Also good to have on hand are a basket with a handle, an attractive box, and a cherub- or other figurine-shaped vessel for more formal arrangements. Containers with a pedestal in china or metal are useful, and perhaps one of opaque glass, since its opacity makes it much easier to hide the mechanism.

Other unusual containers may be obtainable from time to time; some have limited use but are fun to experiment with. Antique containers are useful if you enjoy doing period designs, but these can be very expensive. Items such as Victorian epergnes are very costly, as are vases with crystal drops. I have, however, seen reproductions of some of the antique designs which can still give the right feeling to vintage designs.

Other containers which are lovely to own are the spelter (a kind of zinc) figurines which were used for lamps and have been adapted for usage as containers. The arms on these are usually a bit vulnerable, so care should be taken when carrying them from place to place. Marble containers should always have a supple-

mentary container inside, as the damp can spoil them. Silver is easily scratched, so, again, a lining of some sort is advisable to prevent this.

With accessories the choice is endless; from plastic figurines, which are inexpensive, to Royal Doulton statuettes, which are much more highly priced, all are suitable.

Anything you enjoy can be used when arranging at home for your own personal pleasure, such as a carved wooden elephant or a china swan; but for shows it must be appropriate to the theme. But in both cases, keep away from the gimmicky and garish, for they will do your flowers no favours.

LOOKING AT BASES

Bases in flower arrangements serve to add colour, to give a design visual weight and added texture, to provide further interpretation, and, practically speaking, to raise the design and to protect furniture from water spillage.

Any design that you make should have all its parts in harmony with each other, so avoid putting anything under an arrangement without considering the final effect. As an example, if I were to put a red satin base under a green-dominated landscape arrangement, it would totally lack in harmony, just as placing an elegant arrangement in fine china on a wooden slab would.

From the economic point of view, a base can add interest to your flowers without being too expensive a proposition. For a simple, attractive base, obtain a set of cake boards in three different sizes; those measuring 6–9in (15–23cm) should give you a good start. Simply take remnants of fabric cut about 1½in (3.8cm) wider than your board all around; make a single hem around your fabric, leaving a small opening to thread through with narrow elastic drawn up to fit the base. You now have a removable cover that you can make up in different colours to go with your arrangement.

The bases can be used separately or in conjunction with one another. Straw table mats and those made of thin cane are useful, and offcuts of hardboard or chipboard can be used after being cut to size and covered with stick-on plastics. The woodgrain, pebble or marble designs are best, since they are compatible with most flowers. Felt can be used for Christmas plaques or special colour bases. Teapot stands, or trivets, can also serve the purpose, and the small round ones with legs can be painted black to resemble Japanese bases.

There is a kind of compressed cardboard available at some do-it-yourself shops. This is an excellent material for making bases, as it is about ½in (1.3cm) thick, lightweight and easy to cut. Unfortunately, it is usually only obtainable in large sheets, so you could team up with other flower arrangers to share the cost.

The lids of old cake tins can be covered or painted,

and for Christmas designs you can use hardboard or chipboard covered with coloured foil. On the whole, it is better to keep you fabrics plain and matt, as highly patterned or shiny fabric will detract from your flowers.

As for colour, the beginner should stick to mossy and grass greens, browns and greys. The greens blend in with most foliage, the browns are good for dried arrangements, and neutral greys will look good with bright colours combined with grey foliage. As you become more experienced, you can link your bases to the colours of your flowers.

For interpretive arrangements, bases can be cut in irregular shapes and then painted. Boards dotted with glue and sprinkled with sand are ideal for seascapes, and wood slabs or pieces of slate are ideal for landscape arrangements. A good way to make a cheap base for a landscape arrangement is to cut out a piece of hardboard or chipboard in your required size, using an irregular-shaped pattern (experiment with newspaper until you have something you feel is pleasing, then transfer your paper shape to the hardboard, trace it and cut it out with a hacksaw). Mix a small quantity of filler compound and slap over the shape, leaving some areas rough and some smooth. When it is dry, paint with a mixture of blackboard paint and silver paint, which will result in a pewter-grey shade that makes your base look like slate. (It is possible to buy both silver and matt-black paint in model-paint sizes, but since these are such useful colours slightly larger cans are probably cheaper in the long run).

Other items you could use for bases are small trays, breadboards, rush mats or any plain table mats. Occasionally pieces of marble or glass bases can be bought, which are useful for a change of texture in your collection. Many flower clubs sell flocked or fabric-covered bases in various sizes; cane and rush mats, and wood slabs, are often available from clubs as well.

BACKGROUND MATERIAL

*U*sing long-lasting background material is an economical way of flower arranging. You can employ the leaves of camellia, the swordlike leaves of yucca, and pine and other evergreen foliage, all of which will last a long time. You can then use these backgrounds as a semi-permanent frame for your flowers. Remove the flowers as they go over and replace them with fresh ones. By choosing different flowers each time you can always maintain a fresh look in your arrangements.

Leaves are not the only permanent background that you can use. Dried and glycerined plant material comes in many shapes; these can add interest to a design as well as saving time in arranging. Coconut spathes or palm sheaths are some of the more exotic materials that can be purchased which make an excellent framework for modern designs.

Driftwood can always be used – freestanding pieces are easy to replace and give a different look to each arrangement. Branches covered with lichen provide a framework that looks attractive with flowers; I particularly like this with daffodils or narcissus, as the smooth texture of the flowers contrasts nicely with the rough lichen.

Glycerined beech looks very handsome with orange or yellow chrysanthemums, and the glycerined beech that goes almost black is lovely to use with red flowers.

Ordinary bamboo canes can be cut to different sizes to give a permanent framework for your flowers, and you can experiment with thick basketry cane to make loops and twirls which add interest to designs. Painted plant material is another way of making backgrounds for your flowers; you can paint wood or preserved leaves that are looking a little jaded, and in so doing you can create new and interesting colour combinations.

Metallic car sprays are good to use for pretty colours; mauves, blues, pinks and greens are especially attractive. If you want a disco-type, ultra-modern arrangement, try painting background material with fluorescent poster paints – it's *very* eye-catching!

USING ACCESSORIES

*A*ccessories are anything that isn't plant material. Most people have objects around the house such as figurines, attractive glassware, glass floats, candles

or ornaments of some kind, and, provided they fit happily with your flowers, you can make more of your arrangement with them.

A very good way to cut down on the number of flowers you will need is to place a reasonable-sized figurine in front of a small painted tin can, then to work in your flowers around the figurine. This method will save at least three flowers. Place the finished design on a two-tiered base.

Glass floats, available at seaside resorts, can be used effectively in arrangements. They usually come in mauve, green or blue, and if their nets are removed, they can add a sparkling interest to a few flowers. With their nets left on, you can use the floats with a few shells to create a seascape. These look lovely with soft colours of blue-grey, mauve, green and white.

When using an ornament, bear in mind the following tips to help you improve your arrangements. Avoid gimmicky ornaments, such as those with highly coloured patterns and of very shiny china. Try to use the flowers whose colours will blend in with the ornament you are using. I have a white figurine, and if I use it with any colour but white the figurine dominates the flowers. You will find that wooden ornaments, along with those made of basketry or straw, combine very well with dried arrangements. Brown pottery blends in well with dried materials.

Keep an eye out for interesting shapes and colours in wine bottles; some are most attractive. I like the pottery or stone wine bottles that you can occasionally buy; these are quite compatible with still-life or kitchen arrangements.

ARTIFICIAL FLOWERS

A few years ago flower arrangers would have held up their hands in horror at the thought of using artificial flowers, but the situation has changed with the arrival of silk flowers, a far cry from the plastic horrors of yesterday.

Silk flowers are beautiful in their own right, and have the added bonus of being washable if swished gently round in warm soapy water, rinsed and hung up to dry. They are reasonably priced, and of course can be used over and over again. Silk foliage can also be purchased in many varieties and hues.

There are a few facts you should take into consideration when using artificial flowers to their full advantage:

▌ Use flowers that would normally be in season – don't use silk daffodils in high summer, or chrysanthemums in spring.

▌ Although the arrangements will last, don't keep them for more than two weeks – after that no one will notice them. Either take them out of the container and rearrange them in a different container and design, or store them in a box and make up a new arrangement with different flowers.

▌ 'Cheating' is allowed: use artificial flowers with fresh foliage – they look unbelievably realistic this way.

▌ Make a few curves in some of the wire stems to avoid a stiff look; this will make the arrangement look more natural.

One method that gives you more control over the flowers – it can be used for artificial foliage too – is to remove the side shoots from flowers, such as a spray

LEFT *Using a figurine in arrangements is a good way of cutting down the number of flowers needed.*

BELOW *An accessory is an object that is not made of plant material and with careful use they can enhance an arrangement considerably.*

❧ HOW TO MAKE A POINSETTIA ❧

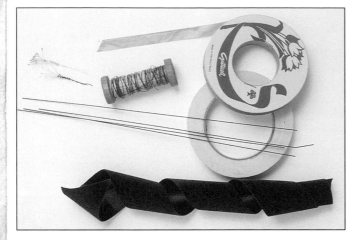

You will need: red, flocked, non-fraying ribbon; adhesive tape; real flower stamens; fine reel wire and sturdier wire; green crêpe paper or gutta-percha.

1. *Cut five, long, tapering petals from the red ribbon.*

2. *Using lengths of sturdy wire, tape one to back of each petal using red adhesive tape.*

3. *Turn petals face upward.*

4. *Using fine reel wire, attach stamens to one petal.*

5. *Add second petal, wiring it to first.*

6. *Bind in remaining petals, one by one.*

7. *Cover stem with gutta-percha or thin strips of green crêpe paper.*

8. *Bend petals out and curve ends over slightly.*

of roses, and give them a false stem with stub wire. Fold the stub wire not quite in half, lay the shorter piece of wire about 1½in (3.8cm) along the stem, and wind the longer piece around the stem and wire three or four times, pulling the wire firm. Then place both pieces of wire alongside each other, and cover all the wire with gutta-percha, a kind of masking tape.

This method lets you place your materials in your design much more easily. It creates a natural effect, too, for you are using the artificial material in the same way that you would use fresh plant material.

I think it is only fair to say that, whenever possible, most flower arrangers would prefer to use fresh flowers, but artificial flowers can be useful – if flowers are very expensive, or if you have central heating, which quickly fades fresh flowers. They are also useful for party arrangements: if one gets bumped against or knocked over, it won't come to much harm. Also, the busy hostess can make up such an arrangement days in advance.

As for the plastic horrors, should you still have any of these left, try spraying them with gold or silver and using them in Christmas arrangements. Strangely enough, you can buy plastic Christmas roses, and because their texture is so similar to the real thing these look quite attractive used with fresh greenery. I have also put some of them on false stems, as they come with a stem length of only 6in (15cm), and some longer stems will give a wide variety of designs. With white waxy candles you can make a pretty design to use at Christmas.

Paper flowers can be made by those who enjoy working with crafts, and fake ones made with foil and fabrics are useful for party arrangements. Personally I wouldn't want to use these all year round, but for economy's sake, don't dismiss them totally.

One paper flower I find useful is the carnation, which has to be the easiest paper flower of all to make. Buy a roll of crepe paper, cut off 2in (5cm) from the bottom of the roll and fringe one end. Hold an end of the crepe paper in your left hand with the fringe at the top, and gather the paper with your right hand while turning it with your left. When large enough, wire about ½in (1.3cm) at the base very tightly, then cover the stem with gutta-percha. This can then be used to make attractive Christmas table arrangements, or to blend with holly, ivy and pine. If you are asked to make the arrangements for a club party, such displays cut your cost considerably.

Artificial flowers are useful for flower-craft work. Try an attractive branch with small flowers glued on to create a mock bonsai; or make napkin rings of ribbon-covered cardboard tubes 1½in (3.8cm) thick with a flower glued on for a finishing touch, or create a hanging plaque of silk flowers attached to a backing of your choice.

Floral and Foliate Plant Material

FIRST THINGS FIRST

ADVICE ON BUYING FLOWERS

FLORISTS When buying flowers, go into a florist shop and sniff hard: if you can smell decayed plant material, leave without buying. This is an almost foolproof guide that the florist is careless about conditioning and looking after his or her flowers.

When you do find a flower shop that smells sweet and clean, then start to inspect the stock. All plant material should look fresh and crisp, and be uncrumpled in appearance. It should look as though it still needed a little time to come out or open up. A good florist will condition his or her more expensive plant material, although it would not be economic to spend a lot of time on the cheap market bunches. The florist will protect the more fragile blooms from extremes of heat and cold, and those placed outside the shop in boxes will be sprayed with water when required.

Although there is a florist in most small towns, it is not the only place where you can buy flowers.

NURSERIES AND GROWERS These generally specialize in only a few kinds of flowers intended for markets and florists, which means that the flowers must be fresh.

At a specialist nursery, such as that of a carnation grower, you can sometimes buy seconds. These are the side shoots of the flowers, not very big blooms, but ideal ones for flower arranging. Very often curved stems, split-ringed blooms, and so-called 'rogue colours' make a flower available as a second. As they are usually cheap, they are a good buy.

STREET VENDORS Buying flowers from these sources depends a great deal on the characters who are actually selling the flowers. Those who are on the premises every day, or regularly every week, are anxious to please their customers. It is true that the flowers are usually more exposed to extremes of heat or cold, but these people generally only buy flowers that are not so affected by climatic conditions. They don't carry such large supplies, and visits to the flower market are usually very frequent. You should get value for money, providing you make sure the material is crisp and fresh.

Often you will find relatively inexpensive flowers in this way – don't dismiss these as a bad buy, for when there is a glut in the market these vendors are able to turn their stock over quickly. At the end of the day,

and particularly on weekends, these vendors generally sell off bunches cheaply to avoid having leftover flowers (which by Monday will be unsaleable). This can prove to be a bonus, as well as a good buy, for you.

GREENGROCERS AND GROCERY STORES   Some grocers sell flowers as a sideline. If the produce is local, it is usually quite good. However, be careful of the multiple stores, or chains, who are often guilty of dumping boxes of flowers in exposed positions where they are subject to extremes of cold or heat.

For instance, I wouldn't purchase flowers such as violets or freesias that have been exposed to a hard frost, so do be cautious when buying all but the hardy species such as chrysanthemums. Where flowers have some shelter, such as a side awning, they are usually protected sufficiently.

As these flowers are generally cheaper than those at a florist, they can be useful when you want to brighten up the home.

GARDEN BUNCHES When out in the country in the summer, you will often see signs outside small gardens offering 'Fresh-cut Flowers'. These are often gardeners selling their surplus stock. Usually presented as mixed bunches, they are great for making a variegated flower arrangement, and as the bunches are usually generous, you can make a massed design.

Often you will discover that these gardeners like to talk about their flowers, and I have received some good gardening tips in these places, as well as pretty flowers. The flowers themselves are generally standing in buckets of deep water in the shade, and those I have bought have always been nice and fresh.

SEASONAL FLOWERS

*W*hen you buy flowers, it is nearly always best to do so when they are in season, for not only are they plentiful and at their peak of beauty, but they are also at their lowest price. It is possible, for example, to buy daffodils in mid-winter, but these are much more expensive than the flowers you can purchase in the spring, and often not as fresh and attractive as the seasonal variety.

The seasons do vary – a cold or wet spell can delay the time the blooms would normally be available – so it is not possible to list available flowers with complete accuracy. However, covering the times of year with the reasonably priced flowers you can purchase within them, in normal seasons the following are what you would expect to find (bear in mind that seasons do overlap):

■ MID-WINTER   Chrysanthemums, snowdrops, anemones, mimosa, violets and tulips.

ABOVE *Daffodil*   ABOVE *Liatris*

■ LATE WINTER Same as mid-winter, with some daffodils starting to be reasonable.

■ EARLY SPRING Daffodils, tulips, anemones and hyacinths. Irises come into the shops now, and although a bit more expensive than the other flowers mentioned, they do seem to last longer at this time of year.

■ MID-SPRING Tulips, daffodils, irises, narcissi, long-stemmed French anemones, hyacinths, ranunculas and wallflowers (Cheiranthus species, or gillyflower). Also small bulb flowers are occasionally found, depending on the florist that you use.

■ LATE SPRING Daffodils are mainly finished, although I have on occasion bought them in the very early spring. Late tulips are still available, and irises are normally as inexpensive and abundant as they are likely to get.

■ EARLY SUMMER Sees the start of the warm-weather flowers, with cornflowers, lilies, sweet williams, carnations, larkspur, antirrhinum (snapdragon) and roses available at reasonable prices.

■ MID-SUMMER This time of year brings scabious, gypsophila (baby's breath), alstroemeria, cornflowers, larkspur, roses, spray carnations and carnations. Sweet peas and lilies are usually at their peak at this time of year. Bunches of statice and helichrysum start to appear in the shops; since these can be dried for winter use, you can use them fresh and perhaps dry half of your bunch for winter use.

■ LATE SUMMER Scabious are usually over, but most of the other flowers that were available in mid-summer are still plentiful, in addition to marigolds, gladioli and dahlias, which start to appear at this time.

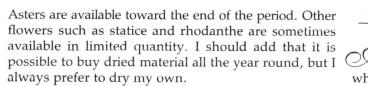

Asters are available toward the end of the period. Other flowers such as statice and rhodanthe are sometimes available in limited quantity. I should add that it is possible to buy dried material all the year round, but I always prefer to dry my own.

■ EARLY AUTUMN Dahlias are in full swing, with a great variety of form and colour, and chrysanthemums are appearing cheaply again; gladioli are still available but starting to go up in price. Asters are a good buy.

■ MID-AUTUMN Chrysanthemums start to come in bunches and are very good buys at this time of year. Spray chrysanthemums are a good value as well. Look out for Chinese lanterns for drying. Other flowers are available but starting to get more expensive. The amaryllis-like nerine and *Schizostylis coccinea*, or Kaffir lily, are reasonably priced.

■ LATE AUTUMN It's still chrysanthemum season, but luckily they come in a wide variety of colours and forms, so there is no danger of getting bored with them. Try the rayonnante or anemone-flowered type for a change. Anemones are also available.

■ EARLY WINTER Apart from our friend the chrysanthemum and possibly small flowers like anemones, this is the most expensive time of year for flowers; but take heart, for if you buy a small bunch of freesias or some of the first daffodils, they will last much longer at this time of year. Sugar-pine foliage is also a good buy, and can form an impressive background for north-temperate holiday arrangements. Holly and mistletoe are available, but the quality does vary according to the weather conditions prevalent during the year. Cones that have been gathered over the year can be wired and glittered, frosted or painted to blend in with holiday decorations.

ABOVE *Foxglove*   ABOVE *Chrysanthemum*

GROWING HABITS OF FLOWERS

*A*cquaint yourself with the growing habits of as many flowers as possible. You will then learn what to look for in a fresh flower. Listed here are the more popular flowers.

■ DAFFODIL AND NARCISSUS These can be bought in green bud, and you can gain great pleasure in watching them open up. In flower they should look thick and be leathery to the touch. If they are papery they are past their prime.

■ CARNATION AND DAHLIA These should look fresh and uncrumpled. The middle should look as though it could open a bit more, and carnations should not be showing their 'white threads', that is, their stamens.

■ IRIS AND ROSE Buy in full bud, or with buds showing colour. Leaves should be green and fresh.

■ TULIP These can be bought in completely green bud. They will then 'colour up', which is lovely if you like to watch them change. The disadvantage is that you can't always tell what colour they will be, but they *do* last a long time when bought like this. If you want a specific shade, buy in tight bud with a little colour showing. Don't buy tulips when you can see raised spots on the leaves; this may well indicate a kind of tulip disease that will rot the flowers and is most unpleasant.

■ CHRYSANTHEMUM Look for flowers that are slightly greenish in the middle with crisp leaves and healthy green stems. Beware of flowers that have been stripped of their leaves, as these are probably not fresh. Provided the flowers look good, however, you could still have them for a week or two.

■ GLADIOLUS Look for flowers with the lower three or four blooms open and the rest of the spike still to come. Pick off the individual blooms as they go over and your gladioli will last quite a while.

■ ANEMONE Do not buy these if they are completely green as they seldom colour up when bought in this state. The colours should be bright and clear and the green ruff should be near the flower. If the ruff is about 1in (2.5cm) away, they will not last very long. Look too for pollen stains on the flowers, another indicator that the flowers are past their best.

To sum up, what you buy will depend on the use you wish to put your flowers to. For colour in the home, a market bunch or garden bunch is appropriate. For a party in a large hall, the less expensive bunches might

ABOVE *Gladiolus*   ABOVE *Iris*

well be suitable. For special designs and show work, get the best you can afford.

Most of all, choose your flower seller with care, carefully inspect the stock and use your knowledge of how plants grow. These combined with common sense should enable you to buy the best for your requirements. Remember, too, to always recut stem ends and condition the flowers the moment you get home.

IN THE GARDEN

*I*f you have a garden you can really enjoy yourself with flower arrangements. Not only can you grow what you need, but you can experience the pleasure of watching your garden grow, season after season.

This section will be directed at those of you with small gardens; if you are lucky enough to have a very large garden, you can just add things as you choose.

Small gardens should include a few shrubs and foliage plants. You will have to look upon buying shrubs as a long-term investment, although it is possible to take cuttings from a number of shrubs. Also, if you go to classes or to a flower club, see if you can swap something you have for someone else's plant material. Shrubs that are easy to propagate are the weigelas – the golden and the variegated ones are very useful. I have rooted rosemary, privet, rue, some of the hebes and Japanese honeysuckle without special equipment. All of these shrubs are very useful to grow; they, along with ivies, should afford you plenty of background materials to play with.

The ivy that I like best is the one called 'Gold Heart', a very pretty one which has lovely sprays and larger leaves to use at the base of the arrangement. It is deep green with a bright yellow centre, and has an added advantage, in that you can pick it in the winter. I grew my original one from a cutting, and I must admit that it took a long time to get going, but it was worth the wait.

If you have a shady part of the garden, grow ferns and hostas. They thrive in the shade, and if you grow only three varieties of fern and three of hostas it will give you a great deal of material to pick from once the plants are established. Personally I loathe privet hedges, but a golden privet grown as a specimen shrub is quite another thing, for not only does it look lovely but also it provides a great deal of material for cutting. I would advise growing those shrubs that suit your own area's soil conditions, taking into account whether you are in the shade or the sun.

If you have a small garden, it is much better to grow any suitable plants that grow well in your area. If you see the plants you want to grow flourishing in neighbours' gardens, they are quite likely to do well in yours. Go for the easier plants rather than those that are difficult to grow, but if you want to experiment with more temperamental specimens, grow them in pots. You can then move them around so that they are subject to favourable growing conditions.

If your garden has a lot of space in it, annuals and half-hardy annuals are a quick way to obtain plant material for picking while you are waiting for the perennials to mature.

A good trick with small gardens is to see how much you can get from one plant. Two annuals that I find useful are candytuft, which provides flowers with a pretty green seedhead that will also take up glycerine; and nigella, which similarly has attractive flowers and a green seedhead that can be glycerined or dried. Honesty (*Lunaria annua*, or satinpod), a biennial, is another great plant for giving a variety of plant material, especially if you can get hold of the one with variegated leaves. You then have foliage, flowers and green seedpods, which at this stage can be glycerined or dried by air-hanging, or you can leave them on the plant until the pods are brown and then carefully peeled, revealing the familiar silvery discs. You can also save the outer husks to create made-up flowers.

ABOVE *Antirrhinum*   ABOVE *Arum lily*

ABOVE *Cowslip*

ABOVE *Lily-of-the-valley*

Another trick is to grow plants that are not easily obtained at the florist. I only have a small garden so I grow white daffodils in it instead of yellow ones, which are easy to get elsewhere. I grow Rembrandt, Viridiflora and lily-flowered tulips, not the more easily bought cottage types. They do not take up any more room, and the bulbs are not that much more expensive than the other, more common kinds, and you will find that you get more interest in your arrangements by doing this.

I like the foliage of geraniums, but I just can't spare the room for them in the garden, so I attach them onto the wall in individual pots. This allows me a little more picking material, and is an idea that could easily be adapted by those of you who live in apartments. City dwellers who have a balcony can grow quite a few subjects in tubs or pots. The larger tubs will take quite substantial shrubs, and if you choose an evergreen subject, you will have plant material to pick from even in the winter months. Underplant with small bulbs or annuals.

I have plants that are special favourites of mine. Of the perennials I include lady's mantle, or *Alchemilla mollis*, a lovely foam of lime-green flowers that goes with just about everything; yarrow, or *Achillea filipendulina* 'Coronation Gold', which makes an impressive garden plant (plus the flat yellow heads dry beautifully), and various heuchera – I have the coral and the red varieties, both of which are useful for pointed material in arrangements.

I also grow quite a few roses, and there is no doubt that the most prolific in my garden is the 'Queen Elizabeth' variety, a pink rose which gives both clusters and single blooms. It goes on blooming for so long that I have even picked flowers from it on Christmas Day. There are, of course, many varieties of hybrid tea roses to choose from with a vast colour range.

I like the curious little *Rosa viridiflora*, and one year I was able to pick flowers from it every single month of the year. I don't grow the old-fashioned ones; I would

love to, but they are generally large and not repeat-flowering.

Lilies are a great favourite, and with so many colours and varieties to use, just pick the ones you like best. Don't forget to plant something for autumn and winter use. I would recommend nerines, which usually flower in October, along with the *Schizostylis coccinea*, or Kaffir lily, a flower that is like a small gladiolus. Dahlias usually last well into the autumn and stick around until the first frost. Chrysanthemums are long-lasting in the garden, and I have found that zinnias and African marigolds last until the frosts.

For real winter flowers, *Iris unguicularis* is a little gem that braves the cold weather. I start to pick mine a couple of weeks into winter, and I can do so for about four more months. Also winter-flowering are heathers; winter jasmine, which provides yellow sprays in the sort of weather you feel it couldn't survive; snowdrops, small but charming, and *Iris reticulata* and *I. danfordia*, both of which will provide winter flowers from mid- to late winter.

If you have room, some small trees can give good material for cutting. Pittosporum – in green, green and white, or bronze – is useful, but it does require a sheltered position except in extreme southern locations. Another small tree I love is *Garrya elliptica*, both for its long tassels in mid- to late winter and its evergreen foliage.

WILD FLOWERS

*S*o many arrangers are what I call 'floral snobs'; they won't use anything that has not been cultivated, and in doing so miss out on some of the most interesting plant material of all – wild plant material.

Now let me make it quite clear that you must *never* pick anything that is rare. Also, I would never cut anything that has only a small clump growing. But a lot of wild plants are so numerous that they are almost classed as weeds. For instance, Queen Anne's lace is so prolific that it borders on the indecent, but what a lovely flower it has! It looks very delicate, but don't you believe it: I used it for a pedestal in a church flower festival, and when the festival was over it was left there and lasted for another week. Mind you, I *did* place it in water with a pinholder and wire for mechanics.

Various yarrows are interesting to use in flower arrangements, and though they are usually white, you can occasionally find a pink variety that is rather pretty. Rosebay willow herb, or fireweed as it is often called (due to its rapid appearance on ground that has been burnt out by fire), is often found growing on waste ground. Goldenrod is another plant that pops up with great frequency, although I believe this is really a garden escapee. Also, there are various members of the daisy tribe growing wild, from the oxeye daisies to the little lawn daisies, as well as a multitude of flowers with rayed petals that are daisy-like in appearance.

A great number of these plants can be found on grass verges by the side of the road, and as most road-side grass is frequently mown, I shouldn't think you would be endangering any species by picking them. Damp places near streams often provide wild iris and arums, and you will often find meadowsweet and forget-me-nots growing in these situations. Berries and hips I mention elsewhere, and interesting seed pods can often be found to use either when they are fresh or in the autumn, when they have dried on the plant.

Most wild flowers lose moisture rapidly, and it is advisable to ensure that you have some means of protecting them on the way home. Ideally a bucket of water is the best solution, but, failing that, a damp cloth or newspaper wrapped around the stems and kept as cool as possible will give them a good chance of survival. Avoid carrying them, as even the smallest amount of body heat from your hand can make them deteriorate. As soon as you arrive back home, recut the stem ends and give them a long deep drink of cold water before you arrange them.

A wild flower that I have always liked is the convulvulus, or bindweed. We used to call this 'Grannie's Nightcaps' when I was a child, and on our way to school we would place our finger and thumb beneath the flower head and say 'Grannie, Grannie, take your nightcap off', and press the large flower, which would then fall off. Unfortunately, when the flowers are out they only last a day and are very fragile. However, I wanted to arrange some once, so I picked them in tight bud, then placed them in a small block of very damp floral foam and carefully carried them home. The next day they were all open, and although it was a short-lived arrangement, it gave me great pleasure.

Foxgloves are plants I am very fond of, and it is easy to grow them in the garden. In the wild it can be found in purple-mauve and white. I prefer to use the smaller flowers or the side shoots as they are much daintier and easier to arrange. They blend in very well with other garden flowers, and the seedheads are attractive both when green or when they have been glycerined.

All of the materials that I have mentioned can add interest to your flower arranging. Try a landscape using oak as a background with beech and a few oxeye daisies and foxgloves; you will be surprised how attractive such an arrangement can look. Or in the autumn try a brass container filled with leaves changing colour and with hawthorn berries and rosehips. You will enjoy it just as much as flowers.

Many wild flowers produce attractive seedheads. You can use these in the green state, or, when they have dried, as additions to your winter flower arrangements.

LONG-LASTING FLOWERS

*I*t is a good idea if you make yourself familiar with flowers that last a long time, for these can be a blessing that you don't have to purchase each week; and though some of them are expensive, their cost is balanced by their long-lasting qualities.

All dried flowers – such as statice, helichrysum and achillea – will retain their colour for a long period of time, and for real economy they are probably the best buys. And you could always make an arrangement with the vivid Chinese lanterns that are so attractive.

However, flower arrangers do like to have fresh flowers. Daffodils can be bought in tight green bud, and if kept in a fairly cool position, they can last up to ten days. It is lovely to watch the flowers unfolding and to see your design metamorphosing before your very eyes. Don't expect the daffodils you buy late in the season to last as long, though, since warmer weather opens them up much more quickly.

Orchids are very long-lasting flowers, and although fairly expensive to buy, they can last as long as six weeks. The smaller spray orchids live just as long, but they are not as expensive to buy. When choosing orchids try to get stems with fat buds at the top third of the stem; most of these will open up and you will know for certain that the orchids are fresh.

ABOVE *Vinca major and stitchwort in a handmade pottery* *vase produces a lovely, natural arrangement.*

A liliaceous flower that is long-lasting and reasonably priced from mid- to late summer is the South African chincherinchee. These will last up to six weeks; just take off the individual flowers as they fade, and every so often recut the stem ends that are underwater to prevent them going soggy.

Anthurium is another variety of flower that is long-lasting, and its bold heart shape, especially on the red variety, makes it useful for modern designs. It is not a flower that is stocked by every florist, but it does appear occasionally at the larger ones, although it is an expensive flower to buy.

The Bird of Paradise (or strelitzia) is another long-lasting flower, which, as its name implies, has the appearance of an exotic bird. They are expensive to buy, but you can make a stunning arrangement with just one of these beauties. If you are offered the leaves take them, for they dry into interesting shapes, useful for contemporary designs.

❧ MORE THAN JUST A PRETTY ❧ (FLOWER) FACE

LOOKING AT PLANT MATERIAL

*I*t is important that the flower arranger should learn the value of plant material as distinct from flowers. Although we always refer to our craft as 'flower arranging', it covers as well the use of a wide variety of plant material.

Flowers, foliage, fruit, vegetables, berries, seedheads, grasses, lichen, fungi, driftwood, gourds – all of these items can be used in flower arrangements for the home. For example, everyone buys fruit and vegetables for the home. It is not eaten all at once, so why not use the odd apple or pepper to add interest or a different texture to your arrangements?

Grasses can be gathered from the wild; so can berries, lichen, seedheads and driftwood. Even patches of waste ground or road-side verges can yield things like teazles, plantains or dock.

Berries are very colourful items. They include the almost-black elderberries, orange wild rosehips and bittersweet, and wine-red hawthorn berries, to name but a few – all these are to be found in hedgerows and are marvellous for making a few flowers go a long way.

Driftwood is so interesting that some pieces are decorative in their own right. It doesn't even have to be found on the beach, for many woods provide decoratively shaped branches or roots when trees are being felled. A good time to hunt for wood is after high winds, when branches have been blown down. Sometimes it pays to remove the bark; this is particularly so with ivy, whose peeled fresh bark reveals smooth wood that looks as though it has been bleached by the sun.

ABOVE *Strelitzia is often referred to as The Bird of Paradise, and though expensive, is a lovely addition to an exotic flower design.*

All found wood should have as much of the loose bark removed as possible before it is taken home (this process eliminates insects as well). Scrape off the remaining bark and dig out any loose pieces, then give it a good scrub in hot soapy water. Paint it with an insecticide for protection against woodworm.

FOLIAGE ONLY

*F*oliage is lovely in its own right, and an arrangement of leaves and stems can be just as colourful and pretty as one of flowers. New arrangers tend to think of foliage only as green, but when they start to look around them – in nature, as well as at florists – they can see the different shades and patterns available.

Rhus and copper beech produce bronze foliage; privet and gold-heart ivy bear yellow foliage; santolina and *Stachys lanata* (or lamb's-ears) leaves are grey, and there are myriad varieties of leaves in green and white. Add to this your glycerined foliage, which gives you brown, beige and reddish-browns, and you have greatly increased the spectrum of colours available.

I have only mentioned a few of the foliages that you can find in these hues. There are more subtle tones as well, like the blue-grey of rue and of some pines. An especially colourful example is a berberis that is purple splashed with pink; and think of the familiar, showy leaves of coleus and of some of the geraniums.

Autumn hues give us yellow, reds and orange, and although they don't last all that long, such fall foliage can make a beautiful arrangement. Even if you are stuck with all green, you can still create a pleasing arrangement; the secret is to vary the shape and texture as much as possible.

Foliage is interesting when strong shapes are used together in a single arrangement. Matt yucca foliage and shiny fatsia leaves, for example, look attractive, perhaps arranged along with some apples (place the fruit on sticks to give them a little height). Foliage and wood are another combination that you could consider; chunky wood with foliage for height and heavy leaves at the base can give you a quick and pleasing design.

When you do have a good selection of foliage, treat it as you would flowers. You can make a background with something ordinary like green privet, adding your more colourful foliage to the front of the design. Focal areas can be a bit tricky to find in foliage, so use rosettes of the most colourful leaves, or houseleek (hen-and-chickens) rosettes.

❧ INSIDE INFORMATION ❧

HOUSE PLANTS

City dwellers will need plant material to pick from to add interest to their arrangements, and it is a good idea to invest in some potted plants. In fact, all flower arrangers will appreciate having different coloured leaves to use even in the winter months, so potted plants are a must for everyone.

You will have to choose your plants according to the temperature of your rooms. Those liking a moist atmosphere could go in the bathroom or kitchen. For those requiring cool conditions, perhaps a spare room might be the answer.

If you have room for only a few pots, I would suggest that you grow those plants that will give you a good variety of shapes and colours, as well as those that are fairly easy to grow. My favourites include:

▮ Sansevieria (mother-in-law's tongue), for its long, bayonet-like leaves

▮ *Begonia rex* and coleus, for their coloured leaves (there are many shades within these two plants)

▮ Hart's-tongue fern, with its wonderfully smooth, straplike leaves

▮ Maidenhair fern, for its feathery texture

▮ *Cissus antarctica*, because it doesn't seem to mind having bits snipped off now and then

▮ Aspidistras, in both the plain green and the variegated variety (even one leaf can add distinction to an arrangement, and they can be glycerine-preserved by laying them in the solution and then sponging them from time to time)

Any of the indoor ivies are useful, as they give trails and from time to time leaves that are large enough to cover up mechanics, and they come in plain or variegated colours.

ABOVE *The wonderful hues of autumnal foliage will donate rich browns, reds and golds to a pure foliage arrangement.*

BELOW *Create variety in an all-green foliage design by emphasizing the varied shape and texture of the leaves.*

You should never strip a plant completely when picking foliage. I seldom pick more than three leaves from any one plant at a time. Always take the most developed leaves where possible, as these are nearer the end of their life. With ivy or other trailing plants, cut so that the plant still looks attractive, but don't overdo it.

Don't overwater pot plants, since more house plants are killed by too much aqueous kindness than by anything else. Give them a feed with some kind of liquid food – usually once a week is enough to keep them healthy.

Plants need not be expensive: you can often buy them at summer fairs or horticultural societies' plant stalls at reasonable prices.

DRESS UP A POTTED PLANT

Flowering house plants are a good source of material for giving colour in the home, particularly during the winter months. It is very easy to pot up bulbs in moist peat, and there is a wide variety of flowers and colours to choose from.

Most bulbs prefer the cold rather than the heat, so don't think that you will hurry them on by bringing them indoors too soon – you could even kill them off by doing this. I usually bring mine inside when about 2in (5cm) of the green shoot is showing, and then I keep it as cool as possible, slowly moving it toward the light. Primulas are plants that become readily available in the winter and early spring, but they do require a cool position and frequent watering.

Cyclamen is another long-lasting flower; I bought one in early winter and it flowered profusely until the middle of spring.

The reason I am writing about potted plants is that, although you are not strictly arranging flowers, you can dress up your house plants very easily by putting the utility pot into an attractive plant-pot cover and standing it on a base. I have a woven china pot that I bought in a junk shop, and it does make even a single hyacinth look impressive when used this way. You can group two or three plants together in a large container to give you a more impressive design. Use a tall plant such as sansevieria (mother-in-law's tongue) at the back, then two flowering plants and a trailing one, like ivy, in the front, so that you have something to flow over the rim of the container. You can easily attend to each plant's individual watering needs this way, for instance, sansevieria will not need as much water as a primula. Try to get the outer container about ½in (1.3cm) taller than the potted plants for the best effect.

If I'm using a single potted plant, sometimes I will place a piece of driftwood in the back to give extra height to the plant and to make it look more substantial. You can see that we have borrowed a few flower-

ABOVE *Indoor garden in a pottery dish with pelargonium, purple streptocarpus, shiny leaved iresine and ivy foliage.*

arranging techniques to improve our flowering house plants!

Many potted plants can be raised from seed. The seed packets often have information as to whether or not they are difficult to grow. If you have a propagator or a heated greenhouse, you can grow a great many different varieties. Even without special equipment I have grown various ferns, geraniums and coleuses, and I'm sure there are many more that are as easy to grow.

❧ HANDS-ON ADVICE ❧

CONDITIONING PLANT MATERIAL

All plant material should be well-conditioned before being arranged. This will help your flowers to last longer. When you are using a supplementary container, such as a small tin can which does not hold much water, it is vital that your flowers are fully charged with water.

For most garden flowers, fill a bucket with lukewarm water to which you have added a teaspoon of sugar. Strip off the lower leaves of your flowers and recut the stem ends. Place in the bucket and leave for at least two hours, or overnight.

At most florists, you can buy a very good powdered product which, when added to the water as instructed, helps flowers to last a long time. I always use this cut-flower 'food' for shows and for special arrangements.

Green foliage should be laid flat in a bath or basin and given a good soak. Yellow foliage requires a slightly different method. Just strip the foliage and stand it in cold water after recutting the stem ends. If yellow foliage comes into contact with cold water it will turn brown, so this is something you do *not* soak.

ticular use to the urban resident without a garden. Occasionally it is possible to buy achillea, whose large round heads dry quite easily.

All these plants should have their foliage removed, and then be stood up in an empty vase to dry them out. With the varieties of statice, I find it best to hang them upside-down to dry; do this in the shade and they will keep their colours all the better.

With helichrysum, it is best to take off the heads while they are still fresh and to wire them with a medium stub wire. The easiest way to do this is to bend about ½in (1.3cm) of the stub wire back to form a hook; pass this gently through the centre front of the flower, and pull the wire until it is just below the surface of the flower. The wire can then be covered with gutta-percha, or straws can be inserted over the wires.

Chinese lanterns are a bit trickier: if you dry them right side up they flop, but if you hang them upside-down the lanterns sometimes hang in the wrong position. On balance, the upside-down method seems the least wasteful. You can open up the pods of the lantern with a pair of sharp nail scissors to give you a flower form. Cut gently and carefully along the raised lines of the pods until you almost reach the middle, and then lightly press the 'petals' back with your fingers. If desired, wire the flower forms separately.

Dried seedheads such as those of the poppy or nigella (love-in-a-mist) are useful additions to your collection of plant material. Both of these can be left to dry on the plant, and picked when they have turned nearly all beige. You can then hang them up to finish the drying-out process.

The method of preserving plant material I like best is the one using glycerine. The recipe is simple, and it results in foliage or seedheads that boast a lovely, silky texture.

The leaves of grey foliage should be wrapped in a cloth with just the stem ends showing. Place them in boiling water and hold them there for about 20 seconds. Then put the ends in cold water. Some grey foliage with feltlike leaves can, if wet, siphon water out of a container, so keep as much of the surface of the leaves as dry as possible.

The boiling method is used on flowers that leak a milky juice, such as poppies or the spurges. This helps to seal the ends. You can sometimes revive florist's roses that start to bend over at the neck by this method. It is also used for clematis and young foliage.

With hollow-stemmed flowers, such as delphiniums, you can fill the stems with cold water and then plug them up with tiny pieces of cotton wool.

DRYING AND PRESERVING
MATERIALS

*D*rying and preserving plant material means you always have something on hand to create a flower arrangement. I have already mentioned that it is possible to buy bunches of flowers such as helichrysum, statice and Chinese lanterns. These are of par-

1 *To condition your flowers and foliage, fill a bucket with lukewarm water and add a teaspoon of sugar.*
2 *Strip all lower leaves away from* the stem.
3 *Recut the stem end and then place in the mild sugar solution for two hours or overnight.*

ABOVE *A popular method of preserving is to immerse plant* *material in a solution of one part glycerine to two parts water.*

You will need one part glycerine to two parts of very hot water, enough to give you about 3–4in (7.5–8cm) of solution in a 1lb (.45kg) glass jar (make up a teacupful to get this amount). Mix thoroughly, then take your branch of leaves, cut the end off the branch and place it in the solution. All leaves that are insect-nibbled should be cut away, as well as any leaves that have holes in them or are otherwise damaged. Seedheads such as foxgloves, dock and plantains can all be preserved in this way. Most foliage will take up the solution well, with beech being just about the best type of leaf you can use.

Beech has the added advantage of being one of the quickest foliages to take. I have preserved beech in four days in a warm kitchen. First you will see the solution darkening the veins of the leaves, until finally the whole leaf has changed colour. With beech you get varying shades of brown, but some foliage, such as *Choisya ternata* (Mexican orange blossom) goes a beige colour.

Grasses can also be preserved by this method, and it is particularly good for pampas grass, which retains its lovely, soft texture when dry. However, you must be sure the grass is fresh and green when you preserve it, otherwise it will not take up the solution.

All foliage should be at its best and fully mature before drying. Young foliage is too floppy, and therefore does not preserve very well. Try to preserve enough different types of foliage to give you a variety of forms. Given a choice, I would preserve beech, rosemary and camellia foliage for use as background material; dock and plantain for points in the arrangement, and choisya and honesty pods for a change of colour (the honesty pods should be preserved while they are still green on the plant). Laurel and *Fatsia japonica* (fig-leaf palm) will provide larger leaves for the base of any arrangement, and I would add a few varieties of grains and grasses and tough foliage such as mahonia in any of its varieties,

along with pieces of cupressus (cypress), which you are often given at flower shops.

Another method of preserving is to dry flowers in a drying agent, usually a mixture of sand and silica gel (a number of proprietary brands can be purchased today). The flower heads, with a small portion of stem left on, are placed on top of about ½in (1.3cm) of the mixture in a box that can be tightly sealed, then the remainder is sprinkled gently around the flowers to fill in all the crevices and completely cover the flower. The lid of the box is then put on, and the flowers are left in the mixture for three or four days, until they have become crisp and papery to the touch. The flowers treated by this method dry beautifully, but there are disadvantages – first, they are quite fragile, and, second, the slightest damp will cause them to flop.

I find that roses in half-opened bud are the least fragile to dry by the above process; they also last longer than most other kinds of flowers. Zinnia, side shoots of larkspur and some of the small spring flowers, such as primrose, preserve quite well, and lily-of-the-valley will provide useful points in your small arrangements. These flowers must on no account be placed in water or into soaked water-retaining floral foam. A dry foam, or for smaller arrangements modelling clay, should be used.

This method of preserving would be of great advantage to those with central heating, as the dry atmosphere keeps the flowers in pristine condition for a long time. Keep all such arrangements out of the sun, otherwise the colours will soon fade.

The silica-gel mixture itself can be used over and over again, if after each application it is slowly dried out in a low-temperature oven. When you see blue crystals emerging, you know that the mixture has been reactivated. Larger flowers may require a longer time in the mixture; you will have to determine this by trial and error. Also, you will need to add false stems to the flowers (wires covered with gutta-percha will suffice).

FORCING FLOWERS AND OTHER PLANT MATERIAL

*I*n mid-winter, I always bring some sprays of forsythia indoors to force, even though at this time of the year they resemble little more than knobbly sticks. I choose the stems with plenty of small buds up the sides, then place them in about 2in (5cm) of cold water and stand them in the kitchen window. I change the water frequently so that the stems don't become soggy, and usually I put the ends that have been in water under the cold tap to prevent any build-up of slime.

In a month or so, the forsythia are usually in full flower. As soon as they start to show colour I arrange them, and then I bring in another lot, enabling me to have a succession of winter blossoms. In the garden they seldom start to show colour until very late in the winter, so that means I have a whole extra month in which to appreciate the yellow flowers.

I also bring in stems of flowering currant (of the Ribes genus). The treatment is the same as for forsythia, but I usually banish this plant to the greenhouse, since I don't like the smell of it when it is newly picked. When they appear, the currant flowers are a very pale pink, in fact, almost white, but the plant has pretty leaves and looks quite attractive when used with tulips.

Hazel catkins are brought in in mid-winter and soon open up in the warm. These are useful for landscape arrangements, or even on their own in a pottery vase. Catkins of the alder are the next to come in, and if the buds of the pussy willow look fairly plump, I bring them in as well.

You may be able to force the catkins and pussy willow about two to three weeks earlier than they will appear outside, but at that time of the year, when flowers are at their scarcest (and most expensive), I think it is worth the effort. Pussy willow makes a pretty framework for a few anemones or a bunch of daffodils, and because you can curve it in your hands, you can make outlines for winter moderns. Curve by placing your thumbs under the willow, and then gently pressing down along the stem until the desired arc is obtained.

Foliage showing fat buds can also be forced. Hawthorn, one of the first to come out, has pretty leaves that nicely complement spring flowers. When the forsythia you have forced has finished flowering, you can take off the spent flowers and let the leaves develop, again providing attractive foliage for filling in the gaps in your spring arrangements.

Aesthetics and Advice for Advanced Flower Arrangers

DESIGN PRINCIPLES

■ BALANCE An arrangement is balanced when the visual weight on each side of an imaginary vertical line through the middle of the arrangement is equal. The design should not appear to tilt backwards or forwards or to the left or the right. The design should not be top-heavy, since the focal area is low in the design.

Darker colours should be used low down near the middle. Place the thinner pieces of material at the top

ABOVE *These lovely freesias are perfectly balanced in a chalice-type vase.*

and the outside of the design, and the heaviest flowers in the centre.

A base can help to give you visual weight, as well as counteract any tendency to heaviness.

■ SCALE (in relation to size only). The size of your plant material should be relative to your container. For instance, you would not place a 'football' chrysanthemum in an eggcup.

The size of the arrangement should be compatible with the room in which it is set up; for instance, a miniature would not be suitable for the main arrangement in a church.

The size of the arrangement should be considered vis-à-vis the furniture around it. You would not, for example, place a huge pedestal on a low coffee table.

The size of individual flowers within an arrangement should be no more than a third to a quarter of the size of their container. Accessories should be no more than about ⅛ to ⅟₁₆ of the size of an arrangement, to avoid their dominating the plant material.

■ PROPORTION This is the relation of size and shape to each other.

The height of the plant material should be approximately 1½–2 times the largest dimension of the container or base. In a horizontal arrangement, the proportion should be about 2–4 times the width or length of the container. In a so-called Hogarth curve the proportions should be two-thirds above the container and one-third below.

An example of bad proportion would be an arrangement wherein the height and width of the plant material are equal, or wherein the size of a figurine equals the height of the arrangement.

BELOW This brass vase echoes the texture and shape of glossy anthurium flowers.

■ RHYTHM Use curved containers with curved plant material, and more angular containers with straight plant material.

Prune out any crossing lines.

Place all the stems close together on your mechanics so that they appear to be springing out from one point.

Use any drapes to follow the line of the arrangement.

■ HARMONY This can be achieved by:

The repetition of material.

Using plant material that grows naturally in similar conditions.

The use of colour blending.

Employing contrasts such as rough and smooth, light and dark.

Selecting correct containers or bases for your flowers. *DON'T* use pink velvet under a landscape arrangement, or put shaggy chrysanthemums in a delicate pottery vase.

■ TEXTURE This is the surface structure that can be assessed by touch or sight; you can have rough, smooth, dull, shiny, velvety and so on.

If you want to increase the importance of a focal area, a few shiny leaves will make it more obvious. In single-colour designs, various textures can add interest to the arrangement.

In dried designs, a few shiny glycerine-preserved leaves can add spice to the long-life flowers.

Remember that texture affects the light play on an arrangement, just as shiny surfaces reflect the light and dull surfaces break up the light particles.

■ CENTRE OF INTEREST The focal area should be under the tallest placement.

Round shapes, or the most interesting or vivid colours, are useful as a focal point.

Use the larger leaves closest to the middle to bring the eye to the focal point.

All lines should converge at the focal point.

Except for sparse line designs, there should be a density at the focal point.

■ DOMINANCE The dominant area in most arrangements is the focal point; a dominant idea can also be used as a theme. Dominant lines, movement, colour or flowers can also be employed.

■ VARIATION To achieve this, use a variety of shapes, colours and textures.

■ GRADUATION The graduation of plant material means going from fine to medium to heavy.

■ CONTRASTS These can be obtained by colour, shape or texture.

THE USE OF COLOUR

*C*olour is an important factor in flower arranging. Not only can it create moods, link up with furnishings and help to interpret a theme at a flower show, but it can also make a personal statement, vis-à-vis the continued use of a favourite shade.

Artists and flower arrangers often use a colour wheel to help them understand colour combinations. However, you must remember that this can only be used as a guideline, for flower arrangers cannot mix their colours like artists or decorators. Flowers have subtle shadings, stripes or blotches, as well as stems, stamens and foliage, all of which may be of a different colour.

The colours on the wheel are the primary shades red, blue and yellow, the secondary colours green, orange and violet, and the tertiary colours red-orange, orange-yellow, yellow-green, blue-green, blue-violet and violet-red. These colours are all obtained from the three primary colours, i.e., red and yellow make orange, yellow and blue make green, blue and red make violet. The secondary colours mixed with a primary produce the tertiary colours.

When black is added to a colour, the result is a shade. When white is added, a tint is obtained. The addition of black or white creates different colours – red, for example, becomes pink with the admixture of white, whereas black added to yellow gives olive green. White, black and grey are considered neutral colours; hue is

the pure form of primary, secondary and tertiary colours, and tones are colours that are greyed.

Again, bear in mind that these guides refer to artificial paints which can be mixed; natural plant material will have to be chosen carefully in order to obtain the colour scheme required in an arrangement.

❧THE COLOUR WHEEL❧

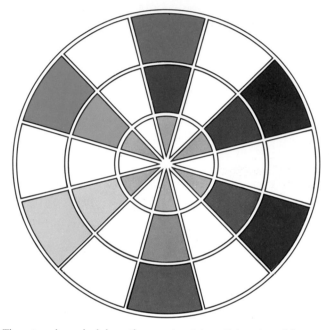

The outer colour wheel shows the three primary colours – yellow, blue and red – with secondary colours (pure hues) in between. The middle band shows lighter tints of the same colours. The wheel diagrams below illustrate four basic colour schemes.

ABOVE *A 'cottage' arrangement: red anemones, mauve honesty,* brown and yellow chrysanthemums, in a pottery pedestal.

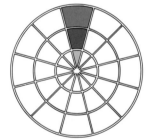

MONOCHROMATIC *Shades and tints of any one single colour.*

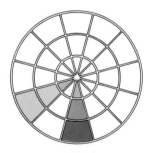

HARMONIC *Groups of any three or four colours lying next to each other.*

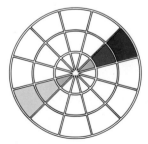

COMPLEMENTARY *Colours which lie opposite each other.*

TRIADIC *Any three colours lying at equidistant intervals.*

Some colour schemes can be worked out with the aid of a colour wheel.

■ A MONOCHROMATIC ARRANGEMENT is one wherein the tints, tones and shades of one hue are used.

■ AN ANALAGOUS ARRANGEMENT makes use of colours adjacent to each other on the wheel, and includes only one primary colour.

■ COMPLEMENTARY COLOURS are those opposite to each other on the colour wheel, and such an arrangement uses these opposite hues.

■ TRIAD COLOUR SCHEMES are those in which the colours are at equal distance on the wheel.

Some colours are considered 'advancing' colours – these are the reds, orange and yellows – whereas the mauves and blues are 'receding' colours. Blues and mauves are not good colours for dark places, nor should they be placed under artificial light, as they tend to disappear when employed with other colours. Red is a colour that is affected by some forms of fluorescent lighting, thus making it look very dull. Reds, orange and yellows are warm colours, while green, blue and white are cool. Colour can be associated with moods, as in the common phrase, 'I've got the blues'.

Colour has associations with various countries, with period designs, with the seasons. For instance, autumn arrangements suggest browns, reds, golds and orange. The feeling that colour evokes can be very useful in interpretive designs, as it can help to enhance your theme. Those of you who like a real colour mixture are using what is called a 'polychromatic' (many-coloured) scheme.

MAKING AN INTERPRETIVE DESIGN

*H*ow do I go about making an interpretive arrangement? This is a question I am often asked, and it is usually followed up by the lament 'But I'm not very imaginative'.

Don't worry. While it is true that no one can be taught to have a good imagination or to be creative, such skills can be cultivated. Probably the greatest key to unlocking your imagination, and to unleashing your creativity, is observation. This means really studying your plant material. Do you notice the shadings of a variegated leaf? This may be the germ of an idea for a colour scheme.

Look at the bare branches of trees in winter – you can see their different forms and colours more easily. Does a piece of driftwood look like a bird, or an animal? If it does, can it be incorporated into a design?

ABOVE *Cerise spray chrysanthemums, pink spray carnations and alstroemeria echo the colours of this old-fashioned jug.*

Start to think in simple terms, such as what flowers would beautify a lady's bedroom – large rough chrysanthemums or dainty freesias? Would a man's study look best with a formal spray of sweet peas and roses, or rugged flowers arranged with pine cones in a strong pottery vase?

Observe prize-winning arrangements at shows; these will help you to understand design composition, and how the flowers and accessories are used to further the theme.

How do I think up ideas? Let's start with a theme that often crops up in a show, a song title. If the overall

theme is 'Songs for Singing', then you have a wide choice. If it is 'Opera', then you will need to do a bit of research. Ask yourself, could I do the Toreador song from *Carmen*, or 'One Fine Day' from *Madam Butterfly*?

Maybe the theme is 'The Sea', in which case a sea shanty would be appropriate. List as many titles as you can, and then reject those that would be impossible to translate to flowers; then decide from what you have left what you are able to do.

If it is 'Songs from the Shows', you will have an extensive range from which to choose, as this subject can provide exciting and colourful themes.

Colour is a factor that can help you to enhance your theme. A blue, white and grey colour scheme would be fine for a seascape, but it would not suggest a circus, which should be a burst of reds, orange and yellows.

Don't use too many accessories, as these can detract from the flowers. Remember that your plant material should always dominate your exhibit.

Sometimes an accessory can start your imagination going. I had a lovely 1930s-style figurine, and when the title of 'Cover Girl' came up in a show, she was my inspiration. This was one occasion when I started backwards and worked out a design that would accommodate the stylish Art Deco figurine. If a striking accessory is your source of inspiration, however, make sure it does not overwhelm the flowers.

A container sometimes leads to a train of thought that can inspire a design. This is particularly true with a modern arrangement, whose container is most often an integral part of the design. So it is worth perusing your container collection to see if it sets the wheels of your imagination turning.

Make sure all the materials used are in harmony with one another: unsophisticated plant material for natural scenes, formal flowers in special containers used with velvet or silk bases for more sophisticated themes. Use traditionally shaped pots without fussy details for modern designs; classic Oriental forms with simple glazes work best.

These suggestions should help you be creative and imaginative in your floral interpretations.

JUST ONE FLOWER

*W*hen funds are low or you just want a simple but striking design, it is possible to create a lovely arrangement with only one flower.

As a rule, a tall container will go a long way to make the most of the flower you choose. The flower should be a fairly substantial one, such as a dahlia, a large chrysanthemum, a gladiolus stem, a half-opened rose or a carnation. You will need some background material, but you should avoid using a mass of foliage, as this makes your solitary flower stick out like a sore thumb. Bare twigs of a reasonable thickness are the best background; use them to give you height, and let them flow a little out of the front or sides of the arrangement.

Another material that looks attractive is alder-cone stems. The stems should have their foliage taken off, which creates a dramatic, silhouette-type background. Even if they are still green, they are quite effective when used in this manner.

Spring foliage that is just starting to bud can be used with a large tulip that has been opened up. This is done by gently turning back the tulips petals at the base (it will not work with a very tightly closed blossom; you will need one that is quite a way out).

Driftwood is a useful background, and its thinner pieces can create a fine framework for your flower.

You will need something to conceal the mechanics, and a few reasonable sized leaves should do the trick. I can usually find one of my various ivies will provide the right-sized foliage. Moss can sometimes work well with driftwood, but if you're really stuck you can always add a few pebbles.

A bud vase can be used for a single flower, giving it a kind of majestic beauty. Cut the blossom about twice the length of the container and add a few leaves at the rim. Place the finished arrangement on a small base.

When you are presented with a corsage, you can very often transform it into a one-flower arrangement. An orchid backed by its ribbon bow can look effective used with loops of willow. Unwind the floral tape from the stem before use; however, if the flower has been wired, just leave the wire in place, since trying to remove it may knock the flower head off.

SPECIAL-OCCASION FLOWER ARRANGEMENTS

*W*hen you are making an arrangement for a special occasion, such as an anniversary, birthday or christening, you will probably want to spend a little more on flowers than you do for everyday arrangements. A good idea to avoid making the arrangement too expensive is to mix a few choice flowers with several less expensive varieties.

Here are some examples:

■ For a golden wedding, you could use a few choice roses and fill in with gold chrysanthemums; add some golden foliage and your arrangement will still look elegant. A ruby-wedding arrangement could feature red roses with a few red spray carnations to fill in. For a silver wedding, white flowers with grey foliage and some loops of silver ribbon pushed in with the flowers would make an attractive design.

■ For an 18th or 21st birthday, use a mixture of flowers in a candle cup on top of an empty champagne bottle, adding a spray of silver baubles (your Christmas ones will do) to represent the bubbles.

ABOVE *This traditional bridal bouquet is composed of lily-of-the-valley, stephanotis and white roses.*

Using your imagination and suitable plant material can be of great help when you are creating designs for special occasions. You can add candles to make your flowers look more important, and any accessories appropriate to the occasion will help to stretch your flowers.

INSPIRATION FROM THE ARTS

Serious students of flower arranging should acquaint themselves with the arts, for they can be of great help in a variety of ways.

Flower paintings are an obvious starting-off point, as their groupings of flowers, designs and colour schemes are easy to relate to your own designs. I have a personal preference for Dutch 16th-century paintings, as a great wealth of plant material was used in these highly detailed designs. You will usually find the designs are square or oval, or have a strong 'S' curve showing through. The containers used in these paintings are also a useful guide when replicating this type of design for an exhibition or show work.

A study of sculpture can heighten your appreciation of line, and some modern sculpture can often be translated into designs with driftwood.

The performing arts, such as the ballet, opera, drama, musicals and films, can give the flower arranger plenty of scope for interpretive work. Just let your imagination run riot: from a simple balletic *Swan Lake* (a water scene) to a more sophisticated *Symphonic Variation* (a modern design), each can inspire a pleasing design. Opera themes such as *Madam Butterfly* might suggest a Japanese arrangement.

Film, drama and literature can be great sources of inspiration; for instance, lovers of driftwood can come up with 'Roots', and succulent-growers can portray 'Cactus Flower' or 'Desert Bloom'. Shakespeare has many themes that can be interpreted, and indeed entire flower shows have featured Shakespearean themes. *Macbeth*, *A Midsummer Night's Dream* and *As You Like It* were some of the ideas portrayed in floral arrangements.

My own favourite themes come from theatrical musicals, with their hundreds of song titles, as well as show titles themselves, proving great fun to interpret. In my day I have presented 'Cabaret', 'Barnum', 'Ipi Tombi' and 'Sophisticated Ladies'. The possibilities *are* endless, so take a close look at the arts in all their forms and create yourself a dramatic flower arrangement.

■ For a christening, a small arrangement in blue or pink with white gypsophila (baby's-breath) would be charming in a cherub-shaped container. For younger children's parties create a design around a favourite toy (but don't forget to obtain the owner's permission first!). They won't mind if you use artificial flowers.

■ For Burns night or Hogmanay, try heather with thistles or thistle-like flowers, or heather-coloured flowers. Add a piece of tartan or a whisky bottle, and you have the basis of an interesting design. Your thistles and heather could easily be dried for this design.

■ For a Halloween arrangement, dark dried material can be used as a background for orange berries and flowers, real or artificial; add a witch or a black cat and you have an effective arrangement.

■ For Thanksgiving, dried material is again quite appropriate, perhaps emerging from a cornucopia basket along with some fruit and gourds.

JOINING A FLOWER CLUB

The inexperienced flower arranger should try to join a flower club or horticultural society, preferably one where instruction in the art of flower arrangement is given. This will help to perfect your own work, for others can point out details you might have missed, or make otherwise helpful suggestions. A club gives you the opportunity to discuss flower arranging with fellow enthusiasts; you can swap plants and cuttings, and increase your knowledge of horticultural subjects. In Britain there are many flower clubs throughout the length and breadth of the land, and many of these are affiliated with the National Association of Flower Arranging Societies (generally known as N.A.F.A.S.), whose rules and standard definitions are accepted at the majority of flower shows. Likewise, the United States, Australia, and European countries have myriad flower clubs. Any flower show will have information on clubs and societies in the area, or just call up a public garden and ask someone there to suggest a local group to you.

Flower clubs vary in the way they operate; some hold classes or 'teach-ins'; some engage regular demonstrators to show different aspects of flower arranging. Most hold competitive shows, and many clubs also run various social functions.

One of the most interesting flower-club activities is participating in flower festivals or exhibitions, which are held to raise funds for churches or various charities. Experienced flower arrangers are often enlisted to help organize various aspects of these festivals. This is great fun to do, but flower arranging can often be rather difficult in these situations, for you usually have to fill huge spaces. This often involves using large props to back up the arrangements, so friends, neighbours and local shopkeepers are asked to lend various bits and pieces. But in the end, it leaves you with a wonderful sense of achievement, knowing you have been part of a team helping a worthy cause.

WRITING SHOW SCHEDULES

*O*nce you become involved with a flower club you may be asked to help establish a schedule for the club show, a task requiring serious consideration. The standard of the club's arrangers can vary within each club, but I have found that most clubs comprise a few very good arrangers, some average arrangers and the rest novices. You should see to it that your schedule caters to all three levels of experience in terms of the themes that will suit the members' respective capabilities.

There is very little point in asking novices for an abstract theme, but they may well be able to cope with 'a basket of garden flowers'. I find the very good arrangers usually like a challenge, so a more difficult class can be set for them.

Some clubs are fortunate to have members who are very good at the flower crafts, and if your club is such a one, try to include a class featuring a picture, plaque or any kind of flower-craft project.

A point that should always be kept in mind is that

the show should be interesting to the public who finally come to view it. If the classes are varied, with interpretive designs and modern or abstract arrangements, as well as more formal designs, the variety will give more enjoyment to the viewer.

I was asked to write a schedule for my flower club to the main theme 'The Victorians', so I did a little research and came up with the following schedule:

■ SILHOUETTE: an exhibit in black and white.

■ INVITATION TO THE BALL: an exhibit to include a fan.

■ A SAMPLER: an exhibit of dried plant material, not to exceed 18in (45cm).

■ OLD TYME MUSIC HALL: an exhibit of natural plant material.

■ READING FROM DICKENS: an exhibit interpreting a Dickens story.

■ THE EARLY PHOTOGRAPHS: an exhibit in sepia, tints, tones and shades.

■ VICTORIAN JEWELLERY: a small exhibit representing a piece of jewellery in natural plant material; a few artificial pearls or stones allowed.

■ FIRST DANCE: a Victorian posy. Ribbon allowed. Fresh plant material.

■ BELOW STAIRS: an interpretive exhibit.

■ MUSICAL SOIRÉE: an exhibit to portray a musical evening.

This schedule gave plenty of scope for arrangers at all levels of ability, with the jewellery and sampler catering especially to the flower-craft people.

The final results were interesting to look at, and represented much variation, with the jewellery class much admired for its intricate work.

When compiling a schedule, the time of the year when the show is to be held must be taken into account. Don't ask your exhibitors for daffodils in a summer show, or for colours which may not be easily obtained. Sometimes in Christmas shows it may be possible to allow the use of artificial material, for at this time of the year, at least in the northern hemisphere, flowers are very expensive and may deter some exhibitors. If they are informed that they can use silk flowers, however, they may well be persuaded to enter the show. Of course, some fresh plant material should be used as well.

When the schedule has got to the rough-draft stage, consult the club members. If the majority strongly dis-

agree with something, take it out. See if anyone has a good idea to fit in with the overall theme; this may well result in a gem being added to the schedule.

Give a little thought to the points I have raised, and you may well find that more club members will be encouraged to go along with you.

EXHIBITING AT FLOWER SHOWS

*S*how work, where it is competitive, is completely different from exhibition work, because you must abide by the schedule. I will begin by stating the obvious – carefully read and understand your schedule. It is no good to produce a beautiful exhibit of fresh flowers and driftwood if you have been asked for an exhibit of fresh plant material only (driftwood, of course, is dried plant material).

Most shows in England are now judged by the N.A.F.A.S. Schedule Definitions, which you should read and thoroughly understand. The United States has its own State Garden Clubs, each with its own definitions. However, it is also true that many small horticultural shows including floral art in their schedules have their *own* sets of rules, which may well be different from those of the N.A.F.A.S. or State Garden Clubs. So give the rules careful consideration when your schedule arrives. For example, one of my local shows will not permit dyed or painted plant material, a rule that might well make a big difference to the exhibit you had planned.

Don't leave your planning until the last minute. Make rough sketches of your proposed designs at least two to three weeks before the show. Check local florists to ensure that the flowers you require will be available. Look for suitable containers and bases. Try out the mechanics and staging, using a tape measure to check your height, depth and width against the requirements of the schedule.

Condition all plant material to be used, and groom all leaves so that they have no holes or ragged edges. Make sure you have all the things you require – a check list is a good idea, since it may save you from arriving at the show minus a vital component.

Take a few spare flowers and pieces of foliage in case of accident, and some spare floral foam and/or pin-holders. It sometimes helps to tie the material for each arrangement in separate bunches, especially if you are making more than one arrangement. Make sure that any drapes you utilize are ironed and crease-free; put them around a cardboard roll to carry them to the show.

Don't take on more than you can comfortably manage. When you are actually doing your arrangement be self-critical: stand back and look at it; can you see any gaps, are there any mechanics visible, would moving an accessory slightly give a better line? If you can see any of these faults, correct them. Then leave well alone.

COLLECTING BOOKS ON FLOWER ARRANGING

*T*he advanced flower arranger should amass some books on the subject. Not only will such a library help your studies, it will give you inspiration for your designs. Don't try to copy, whatever you do, since it is far better – and more of a learning experience – to create original designs. In the case of a specific shape, of course, such as a triangle, you will only have scope for variations in the materials used in your design; however, other people's themes and arrangements may help to trigger off your own imagination.

Flower books are published throughout the world, and they concern myriad aspects of flowers – their histories, their growing habits, their use in art and literature, their symbolic meanings, their significance in various cultures and so on. I am an avid collector myself and have over a thousand books in my collection.

Mind you, I am not suggesting that you should become a bibliophile in order to arrange flowers, but I would recommend that you acquire books on basic design, colour, modern arrangements, dried designs, church flowers, abstracts, ikebana (the art of Japanese flower arranging) and driftwood arrangements, since all of these different styles can be of great assistance to flower arrangers.

Church-flower books are of interest to those who regularly decorate their churches, as they offer advice on the various church holy days and festivals, and the colours that should be used on specific days. Abstract design, like abstract art, is not universally admired, but I find it an interesting and integral part of the flower-arranging scene.

Ikebana is another subject I am partial to – there is a quiet serenity about natural ikebana designs, and I find them restful to the eye as well. I have a soft spot for using driftwood in my arrangements, as witnessed by the boxes of it cluttering up my shed. Decorating with wood gives your designs an individual stamp, since no two pieces are the same.

Some of the specialist subjects will not appeal to everyone, but I firmly believe that to help you to be as creative as possible you must study other people's work. Books on period design are of particular value to those who exhibit at shows. You may not be able to procure the exact, authentic materials (for example, old-fashioned roses, although modern roses with an old-fashioned look can often be obtained), but you can usually create the feeling of a certain period by studying the containers and the types of plant material that were used at the time.

Bookshops selling both new and second-hand stock, as well as libraries, can give you some idea of the titles available, and no doubt you will find your books a permanent source of inspiration and fun.

PART TWO

THE
FLOWER
ARRANGEMENT

he following arrangements will, I hope, provide you with lots of ideas to adapt and build on in order to create your own imaginative and personal designs. You will see a wide variety of flowers and foliage used – wild flowers, exotic hot-house species, many common garden varieties and even silk blooms – as well as many different accessories, all chosen to complement a particular theme, style or colour scheme and to help you find a floral design to suit each season, to cater for every occasion and to enhance any setting.

LEFT *The distinctive shape of these marvellous glossy anthuriums is echoed by the framework of the cano.*

IN A BOX

MATERIALS Box with tin-can lining filled with soaked floral foam. *Alchemilla mollis*, sage flowers, stocks, aquilegia, *Iris siberica*, chrysanthemums.

You can use a mixture of flowers in this design. I have used mainly garden flowers, with a few oddments of chrysanthemums left over from another arrangement. No base is required as the box is heavy enough on its own.

▌ Place *Alchemilla mollis* at the top and sage at the bottom of the can to establish the outline.
▌ Add the fine flowers to strengthen the line, adding chrysanthemums and stock toward the middle and bringing them out over the edge of the box.
▌ Fill in the gaps with the smaller flowers.

When doing a box arrangement, always leave part of the lid showing, so that you can easily see that it is a box.

JUG ARRANGEMENT

MATERIALS Jug, wire mesh. Broom, skimmia foliage, wallflowers (Cheiranthus species, or gillyflower), tulips, chaenomeles (flowering quince).

▌ Measure the wire mesh about 1½ times the circumference of the jug. Crumple the wire up, leaving the cut ends at the top; insert the wire into the jug. Add water.
▌ Add broom, twisting the cut ends of the wire around it to help hold it in position. Insert a piece of foliage to cover the rim.
▌ Add the wallflowers, following the curve of the design.
▌ Place the tulips in position, still following the basic line. Add chaenomeles and a few more wallflowers to fill in the gaps.

A few more pieces of foliage to cover the broom stems would have improved the design.

SPRING BASKET

MATERIALS Basket with handle, tin can with soaked floral foam. Spanish broom, tulips, pansies, wallflowers (Cheiranthus species, or gillyflower), saxifrage, forget-me-nots.

***

▌ Place the tin can in the middle of the basket, and make a low outline with the broom.
▌ Add the tulips on the outside and bring them to the middle under the handle.
▌ Insert the pansies, letting some flow over the side.
▌ Add the wallflowers, saxifrage and forget-me-nots to fill in the gaps.

***

The handle is kept clear so that it can be seen to be a basket, and makes the arrangement easy to carry.

JUST BUTTERCUPS

THREE CHRYSANTHEMUMS

MATERIALS Blue-and-white ceramic cow creamer, blue base, no mechanics. Buttercups.

MATERIALS Pinholder, modern container. Iris leaves, three chrysanthemums.

In case you are wondering what a cow filled with buttercups is doing in this book: (a) buttercups are very pretty, (b) it's very easy to do and (c) the cow is really for the children, to introduce them to the fun of flower arranging. Most flower arrangers find their children are interested when mum 'does the flowers', and this will keep them occupied. Of course, any container and collection of wild flowers can be used.

The three chrysanthemums the florist sent me were larger than I wanted, so I chose a chunky container to add weight to the design, rather than the slender one I had originally intended.

▌ Fill the cow with water, then take a good handful of buttercups, bringing the heads nearly to the same level. Hold them up to the cow, so that they are about 3–4in (8–10cm) above the rim. Allow about 2in (5cm) for the body of the cow, and cut the ends level.
▌ Place the buttercups into the container; they will fall slightly to form their own pattern.
▌ Set the arrangement on a blue base.

▌ Put the pinholder in the container; add water.
▌ Place one long iris leaf at the back of the pinholder to establish the height. Place one leaf cut shorter at the side, and, just to add interest to the form, cut a 'V' out of the tips of the two smaller leaves and arrange them on the other side.
▌ Cut the three chrysanthemums to different lengths. Add them to the arrangement with the tallest toward the back and shortest placed slightly to the front, giving a slight diagonal line to this simple but attractive design.

Don't suck the ends of the buttercups for they contain a poison that can cause blisters.

Any large round flowers and strong linear leaves can be used as substitutes in this arrangement.

LIME AND BLUE

MATERIALS Blue vase, small tin can filled with soaked floral foam. Delphiniums, acuba foliage.

These lovely blue delphiniums were used without any other flower, but for a contrast I surrounded them with lime-green acuba foliage. I could have placed them in a glass vase, but this would have given me difficulty in hiding the mechanics, so I placed a small tin can on top of the up-turned vase.

▌ Place the longest and lightest delphiniums at the back of the floral foam in the can. Add more flowers, bringing them lower down in the design and saving the heaviest flowers for the lowest part. Bring one flower spike way down in the front, so that it will spill over the rim.

▌ Add acuba foliage, keeping it fairly low down in the design.

▌ Stand the arrangement on the blue vase.

IN A GINGER JAR

MATERIALS Ginger jar with lid, wire-filled; scroll-footed base. Bride gladioli, roses, cornflowers, ivy leaves.

- Add water to the wire-filled jar.
- Use the bride gladioli to form an outline.
- Add the roses, saving the most fully opened ones for the front of the arrangement.
- Place cornflowers in between the other flowers.
- Add ivy leaves, bringing one over the rim of the container.
- Place on one side of the scroll base, setting the lid on the other side.

Remember that when you use wire you do not have as much control over your plant material. I would have preferred the gladioli low on the side to have created a curve; then I could have made the arrangement flow down, thus improving upon its design.

GREEN AND WHITE

MATERIALS Green cherub container filled with soaked floral foam, green base. Spray carnations, carnations, philadelphus (mock orange), *Tellima grandiflora* and its foliage.

▌ Make a diagonal line with the spray carnations.
▌ Place heavy carnations toward the middle of the arrangement.
▌ Fill in with mock orange and tellima foliage, bringing some over the rim of the container.
▌ Place the arrangement on the base.

FIVE CARNATIONS

MATERIALS Container with two openings, pinholder, base. Yucca leaves, plantain stalks, carnations, fatsia leaf.

▌ Add water to the container.
▌ Insert the yucca leaves, cut to different lengths, at the back of the pinholder.
▌ Make triangles out of the plantain stalks, and add them below the yucca leaves, bringing one of the stalks out to the side.
▌ Place the carnations in position, putting one in the small opening at the side, next to the plantain triangle.
▌ Add the fatsia leaf to the opposite side.
▌ Place the design on the base.

OPEN-CRESCENT ARRANGEMENT

MATERIALS Dolphin container with soaked floral foam, oval base. Scotch broom, Spanish broom (*Spartium junceum*), chrysanthemums, privet.

———

Broom is bent by putting it on top of your thumbs and gently pressing down.

———

▌ Place the curved Scotch broom in the container, forming a crescent.
▌ Add the chrysanthemums, placing the smaller flowers at the ends and bringing the heavier blooms toward the middle.
▌ Following the line, add the Spanish broom; fill in the gaps with the privet.
▌ Place the container on the base.

———

If no broom is available, look for any plant material with a natural curve.

TULIP IN A TANKARD

MATERIALS Tankard with tin-can lining filled with soaked floral foam. Laburnum, tulips.

———

I wanted to use the last of the laburnum for this arrangement. The yellow spring flower has such lovely flowing lines, but, because of its floppy nature, it is not the easiest flower to use.

———

▌ Insert the laburnum so that it flows well over the rim of the tankard.
▌ Use a tulip at the top of the arrangement, and continue using tulips to form a diagonal line.
▌ Fill in the arrangement with the laburnum and its foliage, and the tulips and their leaves. No base is required.

———

A longer piece of laburnum at the top would have improved this arrangement by providing a little more colour between the tulips.

ALL-GREEN ARRANGEMENT

MATERIALS Cherub container, soaked floral foam, green base. *Alchemilla mollis*, cupressus (cypress), chrysanthemums, muscari seedheads, *Helleborus foetidus*.

___

▌ Place the *Alchemilla mollis* and the cupressus in a diagonal line for the framework.
▌ Add buds of the chrysanthemum at the top and bottom, bringing them through the design so that the heavy flowers are toward the centre.
▌ Fill in with the cupressus, the muscari seedheads, the hellebore and the *Alchemilla mollis*.
▌ Stand on a green base.

FRESH WITH DRIED

MATERIALS Cherub container with soaked floral foam, base. Preserved dock and foxglove seedheads, laurel, yew, choisya, *Grevillea robusta*, beech, chrysanthemums.

___

▌ Insert dock and foxgloves at the back of the container.
▌ Bring other materials forward to create a triangular line, placing the heavier leaves nearer to the centre.
▌ Add a bud chrysanthemum way at the back. Add the remaining chrysanthemums following the line of the foliage, using the heavy blooms at the focal point.
▌ Stand the arrangement on the base.

MODERN CHRYSANTHEMUM ARRANGEMENT

MATERIALS Three-opening container filled with soaked floral foam, tile, fabric base. Iris leaves, plantain stalks, chrysanthemums, hosta leaves.

▪ Insert an iris leaf into each of the three openings, cutting the lowest one short.
▪ Bend the plantain stalks into angles; place one in the tallest opening, and two in each of the others.
▪ Add two small chrysanthemums to the top opening, one into the middle and two heavier blooms into the lower opening.
▪ Add one hosta leaf at the side of the middle opening and one similarly at the lower opening.
▪ Place on the two bases.

This arrangement is mainly for those who like to experiment with plant material. If you have no long plantain stalks, try reeds, which work equally well. You can create your own pattern by varying the angles.

SPRING MIXTURE

MATERIALS Container (Italian cherub), soaked floral foam taped to container. Lilac, tulips, wallflowers (Cheiranthus species, or gillyflower).

I very much wanted to illustrate a spring flower arrangement in this book, but the season had passed and it was early summer, so I was very lucky to get some late tulips. With a few wallflowers and a late-flowering species of lilac, I had just about enough to make this seasonal arrangement.

▪ Place the lilac to give the design a triangular framework, bringing it forward over the rim of the container and at the sides.
▪ Add the tulips, following the line, and then fill in with the wallflowers. Use tulip leaves to help fill in the gaps.

When making this spring arrangement, it would be better to have a little more material – three more tulips would have greatly improved the design.

MAUVE MIXTURE

MATERIALS Bowl, soaked floral foam, two bases. Liatris, irises, aquilegia (columbine), sage flowers, double and single stocks.

All these flowers are mauve, pink, reddish-mauve or purple, which make for an attractive colour blend.

▮ Place the liatris at the top of the design.
▮ Add the irises and aquilegia, then continue the line with sage, aquilegia and single stocks to establish the slender triangle.
▮ Insert the heavier double stocks at the centre of the arrangement.
▮ Place on mauve bases, or use a single base if preferred.

PINK MIXTURE

MATERIALS Marble vase, with soaked floral foam-filled candle cup placed on top. Euonymus, stocks, Japanese honeysuckle, alstroemeria, sweet williams, pink cornflowers, lilac, spray carnations, carnations.

All the flowers in this arrangement range from pink through to pinky-red. Some are from the garden and some from the florist.

▮ Insert some of the smaller pieces of the plant material, bringing some over the front.
▮ Add alstroemeria, sweet williams and cornflowers to make a triangular outline.
▮ Put in some heavier flowers, and add foliage at the back.
▮ Place the carnations, running them through the centre, and then fill in with the smaller flowers.
▮ Set the arrangement on the base.

BERRIES AND ROSES

MATERIALS Tin can with soaked floral-foam filling, base. Privet foliage (*Ligustrum ovalifolium*), hosta leaves, muscari seedheads, *Mahonia japonica* berries, *Alchemilla mollis*, roses.

This design makes the most of a beautiful bunch of florist's roses by adding berries, foliage and seedheads to enhance the design.

▌ Make a diagonal line of privet, and add hosta leaves at the front.

▌ Add seedheads, berries and *Alchemilla mollis* to the framework, keeping the berries lower in the arrangement.

▌ Add the roses, keeping the buds to the top and the sides and the opened roses toward the centre.

▌ Place the design to one side of the base.

ALSTROEMERIA AND ROSES

MATERIALS Bronze cherub filled with soaked floral foam, base. Alstroemeria, *Alchemilla mollis*, roses with their leaves.

▌ Place the container on the base.
▌ Make an outline out of the alstroemeria, carrying some over the front.
▌ Add the *Alchemilla mollis*, following the line.
▌ Add the roses, saving the heaviest flowers for the area near the centre.
▌ Add the rose leaves to fill in any gaps, and to hide the mechanics.

LILIES AND CONTORTED HAZEL

MATERIALS Brown pot with two openings, pinholder, base. Dried stems of contorted hazel, lilies, ivy leaves.

___

▌ Add water to the pot.
▌ Impale the hazel on the pinholder to make a framework.
▌ Break two open lilies from off of the stem. Cut the stem short, and place it approximately at the centre of the pinholder.
▌ Place one lily over the edge and one in the opening.
▌ Add ivy leaves at the top to frame the lily, and one behind the lily in the lower opening (this opening is water-filled).
▌ Place the design on a small base.

YELLOW MONOCHROMATIC

MATERIALS Bottle filled with yellow food colouring and water, candle cup with soaked floral foam taped to bottle, one deep yellow base, one medium yellow base. Spanish broom (*Sparticum junceum*), chrysanthemums, small ivy leaves.

___

The colour scheme is tints, tones and shades of yellow, and my objective was to capture the curving stem of the Spanish broom.

___

▌ Use the Spanish broom to give a gently curving outline.
▌ Place the chrysanthemums lower down, saving the largest one for the middle.
▌ Bring the small chrysanthemums over the rim, along with the broom and the ivy leaves. Use the leaves to frame the central flower and to hide the mechanics.

PINK MONOCHROMATIC

MATERIALS Bottle, stick and modelling clay; pink drape; bottle filled with water tinted red by food colouring; candle cup, filled with soaked floral foam and taped on top; bulldog clip. Copper beech, spray carnations, roses, heuchera, escallonia.

This is a monochromatic colour scheme in tints, tones and shades of red.

▌ Put the stick into the bottle, securing it at the neck with the clay.
▌ Toss the drape over the bottle, forming a triangular shape, and secure it with a bulldog clip at the back.
▌ Add the red base.
▌ Place the copper beech as a background, and then add the spray carnations at the top and sides, bringing some forward at the front.
▌ Fill in with spray carnations and roses, placing some of the heavier roses nearer the centre.
▌ Fill in any gaps with heuchera and escallonia.

The close-up shows the design without the base and drape, still looking quite effective.

ARRANGEMENT ON A BOTTLE

MATERIALS Bottle filled with water and blue food colouring, candle cup with soaked floral foam stuck on top and taped for extra security, scarf as a base. Cornflowers, cupressus (cypress), alstroemeria.

The blue bottle is rather pale, so as an experiment I filled it with blue-coloured water; this helped to make the arrangement look more stable, as you can see from the photograph.

▮ Insert cornflower buds to form an inverted-crescent outline. Strengthen the outline with cupressus.
▮ Add alstroemeria and cornflowers to complete the arrangement.
▮ Place on the scarf, which has been teased into an oval shape.

As this design takes very little material, it is economical to make; any small garden's or florist's flowers are suitable.

PASTELS

MATERIALS Glass candlestick with floral foam soaked in a small candle cup, blue-covered base (Note: the candle cup was stuck and taped to the candlestick). Spray carnations, forget-me-nots, alstroemeria, *Senecio greyii*.

Pastel colours were chosen for this design – pale blue, orange, pink and yellow – with the silver-grey foliage to keep it delicate.

▮ Establish the framework by using spray carnation buds, the longest on the upward side, and the shorter stems for the downward flowers.
▮ Add flowers gradually to the design, keeping within the diagonal line and to the back of the arrangement. Continue adding the flowers, keeping the slightly larger ones for the focal area.
▮ Use grey foliage to fill in the gaps.
▮ Place on the blue base to complete the design.

This arrangement appears slightly heavy in the centre – the back carnations should have been pushed lower down in the floral foam.

LILIES WITH BLEACHED WOOD

MATERIALS Container with spare piece, pinholder, very small container with soaked floral foam, cane base. Bleached wood, lilies, hosta leaves.

The smaller container was made with a spare piece that looked as though it had been broken off of the larger piece. I thought it would be fun to use it as a connecting vessel, so I took the plastic top of a spray can and set it underneath the 'broken' piece.

▐ Put the pinholder into the large container, and impale the bleached wood at the back and to one side. Add water.
▐ Insert the lilies, bringing them to the front of the container. Add the hosta leaves around the central flower.
▐ In the small container, place one lily in the middle, a bud at the top and one at the side. Add one hosta leaf to the side.
▐ Stand both containers on the base, and, using a long piece of bleached wood, thread it through the wood in the large container, bringing it to rest on the small container. This completes the total design.

GERBERAS IN BENT CONTAINER

MATERIALS Bent container with two openings, soaked floral foam. Clipped iris leaves, three gerberas, cut stems of gerbera.

This is a very easy arrangement, ideal for the beginner who wants to start making modern designs. The container should have the soaked floral foam just *below* the rim instead of above, otherwise there will be a problem covering the mechanics and still retaining a clear shape.

▐ In the tallest opening, insert two clipped iris leaves, one at the back and one slightly forward.
▐ Add the tall gerbera to one side, and the shorter one nearer the centre.
▐ Add the gerbera stem to the opposite side.
▐ In the short opening insert two clipped iris leaves cut short, one pointing toward the centre, one at the back.
▐ Place the remaining gerbera so that it is lower than the short one on the other side.
▐ To complete the design, add one stem next to the single gerbera, pointing outward.

PINK AND BLUE

MATERIALS Blue pot and base, pinholder. Painted twisted willow, poppy seedheads, magnolia leaves, cupressus (cypress), carnations.

▌ Insert willow at the back of the pinholder; add water to the pot.
▌ Add poppy heads to the side, and magnolia leaves lower down.
▌ Add cupressus, bringing some over the rim of the container.
▌ Cut the carnations to three different lengths, and position with the slightly larger one in the middle.

Any dried leaves, seedheads or wood can handle a coat of paint and add a change of colour to your arrangement. Yellow, orange or white would look attractive with this particular pale blue.

FLOWERS IN A CANDLESTICK

MATERIALS Candlestick, candle cup, soaked floral foam, base. Singapore orchids, freesias, alstroemeria, spray carnations, hosta leaves.

This colourful candlestick was the inspiration for the design, as deep yellow-orange, white and green are the dominant colours. I have tried to link up the colours of the flowers.

▌ Place the orchids at the sides.
▌ Cut the freesias to establish the height, then add the alstroemeria and freesia to the design.
▌ Insert the spray carnations and add the hostas at the sides and back of the arrangement, bringing a few over the edge of the container.
▌ Place on the base to finish the design.

POPPIES

MATERIALS Brown wine bottle, filled with water. Poppies with their seedheads, buds and leaves; dried wheat.

This design can be done with any flowers for the-arranger-in-a-hurry.

▌ This is a bunch which is grouped in the hand, starting with the seedheads and wheat.
▌ Add poppies and buds, working in more wheat as you go.
▌ Place large leaves at the back, and a small leaf with the largest poppies lower down.
▌ Cut the ends level and place into the container. Tease out gently to space the flowers.

Poppies open very quickly, and only last about three days; singe their ends before arranging.

TULIPS WITH ALDER CONES

MATERIALS Cream pot, soaked floral foam. Bare alder twigs with small cones attached, tulips.

In the early spring, before the trees burst into leaf, it is often difficult to find any plant material that will give height in a design. The alder cones serve this purpose and are in keeping with the way plants grow in the spring.

▮ Create a framework by placing the tallest twig at the back, bringing the shorter pieces down at the sides of the design.

▮ Tulips are added by running them through the centre and to the side of the framework. (Tulips will go their own sweet way and curve toward the light – you can see that some of these have started to come out of line with the design. With early tulips there is not a lot you can do to prevent their curving, although wrapping them in a damp newspaper helps to keep them straight.)

▮ Some of the tulip leaves have been slit at the top and the stalks threaded through; they are used to hide the mechanics.

LUPINS IN BLUE VASE

MATERIALS Blue vase, no mechanics. Lupins.

This is not the best way to arrange lupins, since they are quite heavy flowers and require some support.

▮ Fill the vase with water.
▮ Cut the lupins to different lengths and place them in the vase. (Like tulips, they naturally turn toward the light and then proceed to flop as they see fit).

LUPINS IN WOODEN CONTAINER

MATERIALS Wooden tub with tin can inside holding soaked floral foam, cane base. Lupins.

In this arrangement, you have more control over the design, and I think you will agree that they look more attractive here than in the previous photograph.

▌ Place the tallest lupin at the back of the container.
▌ Bring some flowers forward to come out in the design, and bring one well down over the rim to form an asymmetrical line.
▌ Fill in with more flowers, cutting them to different lengths as you go.
▌ Bring a few of the larger lupin leaves over the rim of the container to soften the edges.
▌ Stand the tub on the cane base.

This is without the base, but with the chunky tub it does not appear top-heavy.

EASTERN INFLUENCE

MATERIALS Small tin can filled with soaked floral foam, scroll-footed base, Japanese-lady figurine. Mock orange (philadelphus), tulips, ivy leaves.

I always think of Japanese ladies in kimonos with cherry blossom, but alas the cherry blossom had finished when I was making this arrangement, so I used mock-orange blossom instead. I stripped off the leaves because it helps the blossom to last longer.

▌ Place the tin can on the base.
▌ Insert the blossom at an angle on one side of the floral foam, bringing it over the other side to form a diagonal line.
▌ Place the tulips so that they follow the line, with the blossom running through the arrangement.
▌ Fold over the tulip leaves and add with the ivy leaves for contrast.
▌ Add the Japanese lady to the side.

I could have used about three more stems of blossom, but it was hard to find any more pieces undamaged by the wind.

ROSES WITH FIGURINE

MATERIALS Small tin can with soaked floral foam, two green bases, figurine. Privet (*Ligustrum ovalifolium*), cupressus (cypress), Michaelmas daisies, roses.

▌ Place the container on the two-part base.
▌ Insert the privet and cupressus into the can to make a triangular outline.
▌ Add the Michaelmas daisies, following the line.
▌ Insert the roses, buds at the top and the more opened blossoms at the base.
▌ Put the figurine in place.

You will note that without the figurine, more flowers would be needed.

IRIS AND FERN

MATERIALS Tin can with soaked floral foam, wood-slice base. Wood, ferns, irises.

This is a very easy arrangement for beginners to try.

▌ Place the tin can on one side of the wood slice, and put the wood in front of the can.
▌ Insert the longest fern at the back of the floral foam, then bring the others to the sides and over the wood.
▌ Cut the irises to different lengths and place them into position with the tallest at the back, along with their leaves. Then bring some lower down in the arrangement.
▌ Add a short piece of fern at the back to hide the floral foam.

The photograph shows the arrangement placed at an angle.

ROSES AND WOOD

MATERIALS Wooden container; tin-can lining, filled with soaked floral foam; wood-slice base. Garden roses, varieties 'Autumn' and 'Orangeade'.

▌ Place the wooden container onto the wooden slice.
▌ Insert a tall bud at the back of the floral foam, then add more roses with the buds at the top, making a near-vertical arrangement.
▌ Bring the heavier roses closer to the middle, placing a bud to one side of the arrangement.
▌ Add rose leaves to fill in the gaps and hide the mechanics.

There are many excellent varieties of rose you can use for flower arranging. If I only had room for one bush, I would grow 'Queen Elizabeth', a rich pink variety which has lovely long stems, some of which produce single flowers, others clusters of flowers.

IN AN ENGLISH COUNTRY GARDEN

MATERIALS Two large stones, cotton birds, slate base, tin can with soaked floral foam. Campanula (bellflower), stocks, pontilla, sweet peas, pinks, aquilegia (columbine), scabious, linaria, honeysuckle, hebe, cupressus (cypress), achillea.

▌ Using the campanula, start at the top to create an asymmetrical line.
▌ Add the mixed flowers to follow the line. Save the heavy flowers for the base.
▌ Insert the cupressus at the back and fill in the gaps with hebe and additional cupresses.
▌ Place on the base and arrange the stones at one side.
▌ Add the cotton birds to complete the picture.

Although this arrangement does not contain all the flowers mentioned in the song 'An English Country Garden', it represents a good mixture nonetheless. Any assortment from your garden – English or any other nationality – can be used as available.

CURVED ARRANGEMENT
IN FIGURINE

MATERIALS Figurine with screw-on candle cup filled with soaked floral foam. Box foliage, stocks, sweet peas, spray carnations, roses, scabious.

▌ Insert a long piece of the curved box foliage to one side, and a shorter piece at the other.
▌ Place the sweet peas and spray carnations at the top, making a curved outline.
▌ Fill in with the smaller flowers, adding the heavy ones in the middle.
▌ Bring some flowers forward over the rim, letting them flow down.
▌ Fill in the gap with short flowers and small pieces of foliage.

Any mixture of similar flowers can be used in this pleasing design.

| ALL-FOLIAGE ARRANGEMENT | PINK FLOWERS WITH GLASS |

MATERIALS Cherub with soaked floral-foam base. Privet, euonymus, oak, griselinia, acuba, aquilegia (columbine), cupressus (cypress), rue, *Senecio greyii*.

This arrangement uses a variety of foliage chosen for both their colour and their texture. As you can see, they make quite a colourful arrangement.

■ The first placement of privet goes to one side of the arrangement.
■ Add the green and white euonymus at the opposite side.
■ Add foliage to keep the asymmetrical line, with the heaviest and most colourful leaves placed near the middle of the arrangement, thereby creating a focal point.
■ Place the arrangement on the base.

MATERIALS Bottle with stick secured inside with modelling clay, pink drape, small tin can with soaked floral foam, two glass stands, glass base, glass baubles. Lilies, *Dicentra formosa*, cornflowers, scabious, stocks, sweet peas, sweet williams, spray carnations.

This design consists of a mixture of pink-toned flowers, most of which came from the garden. Colour linking is also a good way of enhancing florist's flowers. The glass helped to add a different texture.

■ Arrange the drape in a triangular shape over the stick-filled bottle.
■ Put the glass base on to the stands, and the tin can on one side of the base.
■ Make a framework, starting with the tallest flower following the line of the drape.
■ Add the flowers to fill the centre, top and sides.
■ Place the heavy flowers in the middle, and fill in with short-stemmed flowers to hide the mechanics.

'SWAN LAKE'

HAWAIIAN MEMORIES

MATERIALS Kidney-shaped dish, pinholder, adhesive clay, pebbles, swan. *Typhus augustifolia* (known as reedmace, cat's-tails or bulrush), irises, hosta leaves, moss.

A simple arrangement, suitable for a beginner.

▌ Place the pinholder to one side of the dish, sticking it down with adhesive clay. Make sure both the dish and container are dry. Then, when it is firmly secured, add water to the dish.
▌ Insert the bulrushes cut to different lengths at the back of the pinholder.
▌ Place a bud iris near the top of the bulrushes, and a slightly shorter one to one side. Place the remaining three irises near the centre and centre sides.
▌ Fill in with iris leaves. Add hosta leaves near the base.
▌ Arrange the pebbles to conceal the pinholder, then spread a little moss over any bits still showing.
▌ To complete the picture, place the swan on the opposite side from the flowers.

Any water-loving plant can be used in this arrangement.

MATERIALS Tin can with soaked floral foam, Hawaiian god, wood-slice base. Poinciana pods, cymbidium and Singapore orchids, lily-of-the-valley leaves, jacaranda pods, various dried pods.

We all like to bring back souvenirs from our holidays. I go around collecting dried-plant material, all of which used in this arrangement came from Hawaii (along with the figure of Lono, the Polynesian god of peace and prosperity). If you have a favourite souvenir, try incorporating it into an appropriate flower arrangement.

▌ Place a long curving poinciana pod at the side of the container, and another at the base to give a crescent outline.
▌ Insert the Singapore orchids at the top and bottom, then add more small orchids along with the cymbidium and twisted pods in the middle.
▌ Add lily-of-the-valley leaves at the leaves at the back, and a few orchids over the rim of the container.
▌ Add a few jacaranda pods low down and at the base with other dried pods.
▌ Place on the base and stand Lono on one side to finish the picture.

TWO-TIER FOLIAGE
ARRANGEMENT

MATERIALS Wrought-iron container filled with two small tin cans containing soaked floral foam, green base. Assorted foliage, including berberis, weigela, lonicera, privet, cupressus (cypress), rue, euonymus.

▌ For the top of the arrangement, use curving pieces of the plant material, following the line of the container.
▌ Add small snippets of foliage, working in various colours and textures as you go. Add the brightest colours at the centre.
▌ For the lower part, make a horizontal line with the lonicera, and add small pieces to fill in, using the most vivid hues at the front.
▌ Place the finished design on the green base.

AUTUMN CONCERTO

MATERIALS Tin can with soaked floral foam, wooden-slab base, two robins. Preserved plant material, chrysanthemums, wood, artificial rosehips.

This autumnal arrangement has the two robins giving a concerto. I had to cheat and use artificial rosehips, but they combine quite well with the rest of the plant material.

▌ Place the container to one side of the base.
▌ Place the preserved plant material at the back, and use the chrysanthemums to create an asymmetrical line.
▌ Add the piece of wood to one side, and bring the chrysanthemums forward to come slightly over the rim.
▌ Fill in with more chrysanthemums, and place berries throughout the design.
▌ Add a few segments of preserved material to fill in at the base.
▌ Arrange the birds to one side to complete.

ODDS AND ENDS

MATERIALS Orange candle in candle holder, tin can with soaked floral foam, oval base. *Euonymus japonicus*, spray carnations, lilies.

This design was created from oddments left in the flower bucket. As they were all orange-coloured flowers, I felt that the colour link would help to blend even the rather large lilies with the small spray carnations. The ornamental candle was used to give a little more colour impact – it is not intended to be lit.

▌ Put the candle holder in the middle of the floral foam.
▌ Make a low outline with the euonymus and the spray carnations.
▌ Add the lilies, keeping them recessed and low down in the arrangement.
▌ Fill in with short sprays of euonymus and carnations.
▌ Place on the base, and put the candle into the holder.

LAMP ACCESSORY

MATERIALS Tin can with soaked floral foam, oval base, lamp. Chrysanthemums, privet.

▌ Starting with the tallest buds of the chrysanthemums, place them at the back of the container.
▌ Add the privet to hide the rather 'leggy' stem.
▌ Bring more of the chrysanthemums down to make an asymmetrical line, with the buds at the bottom and the heavy flowers at the centre.
▌ Fill in the gaps with privet and more chrysanthemums.
▌ Place on the base, adding the lamp to one side.

BLUE AND WHITE

MATERIALS Tin can with soaked floral foam, blue base, figurine. Bride gladioli, delphiniums, Singapore orchids.

The Art Deco-style figurine was the inspiration for this arrangement. She is rather pretty, and makes a nice addition to a floral grouping.

▌ Using the bride gladioli, make an asymmetrical outline.
▌ Place the delphiniums into the container, saving the heavy ones for the middle.
▌ Add the Singapore orchids, with some at the back and a few at the front and over the rim of the container.
▌ Hide the mechanics with delphinium leaves, bringing some over the edge of the container.
▌ Place the arrangement on the base, and add the figurine to one side.

If you have a favourite statuette, use it in an arrangement, linking its colour(s) to those of your flowers.

MAUVE WOOD WITH LILIES

MATERIALS Painted tin can, pinholder, mauve base. Mauve-painted wood, ivy leaves, two stems of lilies.

This is an economical arrangement to make, as the painted wood can serve as a background for other flowers when the lilies have finished. The very twisted wood was acquired from a flower-club sales table. It was rather shabby, so I sprayed it, as well as the straight piece, with a mauve metallic car spray. The lilies were brought into the warm to open them up a bit.

▌ Place the tin can containing the pinholder on to the mauve base. Impale the wood on the pinholder. Add the ivy leaves at the base, as well as some water.
▌ Take an open lily off one of the stems. Place the tall stem near the wood, and add the shorter stem lower down, bringing it slightly forward.
▌ Add the single lily low down in the front.

ONE GLADIOLUS

MATERIALS Rose bowl, pinholder, adhesive clay. One gladiolus with leaves, three ivy leaves, three pieces of contorted willow.

▌ Stick the pinholder in the bowl with the adhesive clay.
▌ Impale the two larger pieces of willow on the pinholder to make a framework.
▌ Place the gladiolus in the centre with the leaves.
▌ Add ivy at the base, along with the small piece of willow to complete the design.

A ONE-FLOWER ARRANGEMENT

MATERIALS Pinholder, corsage ribbon, homemade black container, small base. Willow loops, hosta leaves, ferns, orchid.

When you receive a corsage, it seems a shame to put the lovely flower into a small pot. To use it to its best advantage, feature it in a one-flower arrangement, like the one illustrated.

▌ Make loops of willow by tying them down with thread, then place them at the back of the pinholder.
▌ Add a frame of hosta leaves in the centre of the pinholder.
▌ Add the orchid with its ribbon backing to the front of the arrangement, bringing it slightly over the rim of the container.
▌ Stand the arrangement on a small base.

The container is a painted bleach bottle with a small tin can fitted into the top.

DOWN BY THE RIVERSIDE

MATERIALS Large container, pinholder, large stone, duck. *Typha augustifolia* (known as bulrush, lesser reedmace, cat's-tails), flags (*Iris pseudacorus*), hosta leaves.

This arrangement is a small-scale river scene. Use a container that will give you a wide area for water.

▌ Insert the bulrushes, cut to different heights, at the back of the pinholder.
▌ Add the iris leaves to create a framework.
▌ Put the irises in the centre, adding a few to the sides and front of the arrangement.
▌ Place the hosta leaves at the bottom, and arrange the large stone to hide the mechanics.
▌ Fill the container with water, and set the duck at the side opposite the flowers.

Other accessories that could be used in such an arrangement are frogs and herons, or perhaps a figurine of a child fishing.

WILD FLOWERS AND WOOD

MATERIALS Wooden container, wood-slice base, soaked floral foam. Dock, oxeye daisies (*Chrysanthemum leucanthemum*), grass, clover (*Trifolium pratense*).

I acquired the large knee-shaped wood with container attached at a car boot sale for the great sum of 50 pence (under $1) – what a bargain! I used light brown shoe polish to add a little colour to the wood, then along with another wood piece I owned, it was ready for use.

▌ Place the tallest dock at the back of the floral foam.
▌ Insert the daisies and the grass, bringing them along with the clover through the design.
▌ Insert a few large daisies and pieces of dock to flow over the front.
▌ Fill in with a few more pieces of grass to add a change of texture.
▌ Place on the wooden slice.

Any wild flowers with wood can be used, but do make sure they are not on a conservation list.

WALK IN THE WOODS

MATERIALS Large tin can with soaked floral foam, wood slice, hollow log, very small tin can with soaked foam in the log. Oak, clover, dog roses, ferns.

▌ Place the large tin can on the wood slice, with the log on the opposite side and the small can partially inside the log.

▌ Insert the oak in the large container for the background, and bring the shorter pieces to the side and over the rim.

▌ Add the clover to one side, and the dog roses to the other side and the centre, bringing them well over the rim of the container to completely conceal it.

▌ Arrange the ferns in the small can so that they look like a growing clump.

WILD FLOWERS IN WOODEN TUB

MATERIALS Wooden tub; tin can for inner lining, filled with well-soaked oasis. Tansy leaves, charlock (*Sinapsis arvensis*), cow parsley (Queen Anne's lace), ragwort (*Senecio squalidus*), sowthistle (*Sonchus arvensis*), oxeye daisies (*Chrysanthemum leucanthemum*).

▌ Insert the tansy leaves so that they flow over the edge of the container; add a few in the middle.

▌ Make an outline with the charlock and cow parsley, placing a stem of sowthistle lower down at one side.

▌ Add the daisies; run them through the design using the largest near the centre.

This is virtually a collection of road-side weeds, thus creating a very economical arrangement. Use any that are prolific in your locality to make a similar arrangement.

ORCHIDS, FERNS AND FIGURINE

MATERIALS Base, painted tin can, soaked floral foam, figurine. Iris leaves, ivy, nephrolepsis ferns, orchids.

▌ Place the container on the base. Insert the iris leaves at the back and the ivy at the bottom, bringing some over to cover the can.

▌ Add the ferns to give an asymmetrical line.

▌ Place the orchid sprays so that they run through the design, bringing some forward to the front of the arrangement.

▌ Set the figurine to one side of the arrangement to complete the picture.

The ferns were 'lifted' from a potted plant for this design. As it was a fairly substantial fern, I was able to take quite a few without injuring the plant.

MODERN WITH WOOD
AND GERBERAS

MATERIALS Tall container, filled with soaked floral foam. Three thin pieces of driftwood, three gerberas, two large ivy leaves.

▊ Balance a piece of driftwood on the rim of the container, and push a long piece straight down on the oasis. Push the other piece into the foam so that it comes over the rim of the container.
▊ Insert the gerberas, which have been cut to different lengths; place the centre one low in the arrangement.
▊ Back the flowers with an ivy leaf, and bring the other leaf over the rim.

Flowers such as medium-large chrysanthemums, or in the summer open roses, also would be suitable for this design. As the framework is permanent, you could keep if going for a long time – just replace the flowers as they go over.

DRIFTWOOD WITH
CHRYSANTHEMUMS

MATERIALS Pinholder in a small tin can, wood-slice base. Driftwood, chrysanthemums, hosta leaves.

Here's another economical and long-lasting arrangement, using just seven flowers. The rather handsome piece of driftwood is a favourite of mine.

▊ Add some water to the container, and impale the wood on the pinholder.
▊ Place two of the chrysanthemums behind the wood.
▊ Bring two of the flowers in front to form a straight line, then swing the other three over to the opposite side in a slight curve.
▊ Place the arrangement on the base.
▊ Add a small piece of driftwood to hide the container, and a few hosta leaves to add a little weight at the base.

Any medium-sized flowers could be used for this arrangement.

LILIES AND WOOD

MATERIALS Small tin can filled with soaked floral foam, wooden base. Driftwood, two stems of lilies, griselinia foliage.

———

This is an economical arrangement which is also long-lasting. The large piece of driftwood is nailed to a thin wooden slice, which makes it freestanding. It has room for the small tin can underneath.

———

▌ Place the wood on the base with the container in position.
▌ Add one stem of lilies at the back of the wood.
▌ Break off one open lily from the second stem, then put the remainder, cut quite short, in front of the wood. Place the single lily at the side lower down.
▌ Add the foliage to the front to hide the mechanics. Put the small piece of wood in front of the container.

———

If you take off the lilies as they finish on the stems, it will encourage the other buds to open up.

CARNATIONS WITH FASCIATED WOOD

MATERIALS Pinholder, pottery container. Fasciated wood, carnations, acuba foliage.

———

I love fasciated wood, and in this arrangement I have used it with just a few flowers so that its interesting outline can be seen.

———

▌ Place the tallest piece of wood on the back of the pinholder in the water-filled container. Add the shorter pieces at the side, bringing them slightly forward.
▌ Cut the five carnations to different lengths, adding the tallest at the back and the shorter ones to the front of the arrangement, bringing them over the rim of the container.
▌ Place the carnation foliage to the centre and to one side.
▌ Add a short piece of acuba, bringing it over the rim.

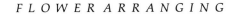

GERBERAS

MATERIALS Black-painted tin can, pinholder, black-covered base. Black-painted wood, three gerberas, fatsia leaf, moss.

This arrangement makes the most of three large flowers. The wood serving as a background can also be used as a frame for other flowers once the gerberas are finished.

▌ Impale the wood on the pinholder, which has been placed in the water-filled container. Cut the gerberas to different lengths, using the cut stems on one side.
▌ Place the flowers with the longest stem against the wood, the next flower to the side opposite the stems, and the third brought nearer to the middle.
▌ Add a fatsia leaf at the base.
▌ Cover the pinholder with a small amount of moss.
▌ Place the arrangement on the black base.

CHRYSANTHEMUMS, WOOD AND BULRUSHES

MATERIALS Tin can with pinholder, small piece of soaked floral foam at front and back of wood, cane base. Wood, bulrushes, chrysanthemums, acuba foliage.

This arrangement was made to show off the flat piece of wood – it's one of the pieces I like to play with. I would have preferred marguerites, but none were available, so I used chrysanthemums as a substitute.

▌ Press the wood firmly on to the pinholder.
▌ Place the bulrushes at the back of the wood, along with two of the chrysanthemums.
▌ Bring the rest of the flowers in front of the wood, with one spray to the side.
▌ Place the container on the cane base; add a piece of wood in front of the can.
▌ Add acuba foliage to hide the mechanics and finish the design.

DRESS UP A POTTED PLANT

MATERIALS Potted plant (kalanchoe), base, china pot, piece of cane formed into a loop.

———————

This is a simple idea for the arranger in a hurry. It is not strictly a flower arrangement, but it uses some of the art's techniques.

———————

▌ Start with the plant placed in the china pot.
▌ Place the plant on the base.
▌ Add a loop of cane. Now that it's complete it looks *much* more interesting.

———————

For a variation, you could put a long narrow piece of driftwood into the soil at the back of the plant, preferably one with an interesting shape. Then hang a small piece of wood over the sides.

CANE LOOP WITH CARNATIONS

MATERIALS Homemade container, tin can with soaked floral foam, green base. Cane loops, spray carnations, hosta leaves.

———

▌ Place the hoops in the container, with the tallest at the back.
▌ Cluster the carnations at the front, most of them cut fairly short, but with a few long ones up at the back.
▌ Add hosta leaves, taking one up at the back and bringing one low down over the container. Add the other leaves between the flowers.
▌ Place on the green base.

———

The container is a bleach bottle that has been filled with filler compound that has been allowed to dry; a small tin can rests on the top. The bottle is then painted white.

BLACK AND ORANGE

MATERIALS Black homemade container with two openings, soaked floral foam, pinholder, base. Black-painted wood, palm leaves, lilies, poppy seedheads, magnolia leaves.

———

▌ Put the floral foam into the top opening of the container, and place a small pinholder in the lower.
▌ For the top placement insert the wood and palm leaves to make a background, and bring one large leaf over the rim of the container. Insert the lilies, bringing the open flowers to the centre. Fill in with the poppy heads and magnolia leaves.
▌ For the bottom placement, place a dry leaf on the pinholder. Add the lilies and some water.
▌ Stand the container on the base, putting a piece of wood in front of the container to complete the design.

FERNS AND FOXGLOVES

MATERIALS Large container, pinholder. Male fern (*Dryopteris Filix-mas*), foxgloves (*Digitalis purpurea*), moss.

———

I like the combination of fern and foxgloves. These are often found on the fringes of woodlands, although I grow both of them in my garden.

———

The container is homemade; it was a large, old-fashioned meat dish bought at a jumble sale. I covered its sides with a fairly stiff mixture of filling compound, then roughed it up with a fork. When dry, it was painted with a combination of silver and blackboard paints.

———

▪ Make a background of ferns on the pinholder, with the tallest at the back.
▪ Add the tallest foxglove near the tallest fern.
▪ Cut the other foxgloves to different lengths, bringing some slightly to the front with the shorter fern.
▪ Use a little moss to hide any mechanism.
▪ Fill the container with water.

DRIED DESIGN

MATERIALS Pottery jar, dry floral foam. Echinops, mahonia, beech, dock, plantain, foxglove seedheads, eucalyptus, grevillea foliage, molucella, achillea, Chinese lanterns.

———

▪ Insert the various seedheads at the back to form a background. Place mahonia, beech and grevillea on the outside and over the edge of the container.
▪ Fill the centre with echinops, molucella, Chinese lanterns and achillea, bringing the heaviest pieces toward the lower centre.

———

No base is required for this design as the jar is heavy enough to give it visual weight.

ORCHIDS WITH HOSTAS

MATERIALS Rose bowl, pinholder. Iris leaves, hosta leaves, orchids, ivy leaves, acuba foliage.

▌ Insert the iris leaves at the back of the pinholder in the bowl; add water.
▌ Add the hosta leaves, bringing them to the side and front.
▌ Put the orchids in the middle of the arrangement.
▌ Fill in with the ivy, and bring the acuba foliage over the rim of the container to finish the arrangement.

JUST THREE ALLIUMS

MATERIALS Bowl, pinholder. Cut iris foliage, three alliums, magnolia leaves.

The three alliums were all obligingly at different stages of their development, so that I had a small, medium and large bloom to work with.

▌ Insert the three iris leaves, two of them cut straight at the top, at the back of the pinholder, which has been set in a shallow bowl of water.
▌ Put in the alliums, graduating the sizes so that the small bloom is at the top, the medium at the centre and the large at the base.
▌ Hide the mechanics with the magnolia leaves.

When the alliums are finished in your arrangement, hang them upside-down in a dark airy place to dry. They are useful additions to your dried-material collection.

ANTHURIUMS

MATERIALS Bowl, pinholder. Cane, anthuriums, large ivy leaves.

Anthuriums are such dramatic flowers that it is difficult to know what to use them with, so I settled for cane just to emphasize their form.

▌ In the pinholder, which is resting in a shallow, water-filled bowl, place the cane at the back and slightly forward.

▌ Insert the tallest flower at the back, and bring the next two flowers lower down, framing them with the cane loop.

▌ Put the last two flowers lower down in the arrangement.

▌ Cover the mechanics with ivy leaves.

AGAPANTHUS

MATERIALS Tall brown and lime-green container, soaked floral foam. Acuba foliage, agapanthus.

This design makes the most of three agapanthus; even the stems are used to assist in the design. Some of the acuba foliage has been pruned off the larger leaves to give a better line.

▮ Place a long stem of trimmed acuba in the centre of the foam, which has been put into the container. Add short pieces, bringing them to the front.
▮ Cut the agapanthus to different lengths. Add the cut portions of the stems at the back and to one side.
▮ Put in the three agapanthus – two at the back and the shorter one to the front.
▮ No base is needed for this design.

ORCHIDS, FERN AND WILLOW

MATERIALS Plastic container, pinholder, small base. Iris leaves, willow, Singapore orchids, cymbidium orchid, fern.

———

▪ Place the iris leaves at the back of the water-filled container to establish height.
▪ Loop the willow with strong thread and place it in front of the iris leaves with some of the loops to one side.
▪ Add the Singapore orchids in a casual manner, bringing some of them lower down and to the front of the arrangement.
▪ Use the cymbidium as a focal point; add the ferns.
▪ Place on the base to complete the design.

———

The base has been chosen for the colour link to the Singapore orchids, but it would look just as well on a moss-green base.

SILK CORNFLOWERS

MATERIALS Container with dried foam. Silk fern, cornflowers, daisies, ivy; dried wheat, plastic fern.

———

Silk flowers are mixed with dried wheat to give a country feeling to the arrangement. The wooden container, which looks like bark, enhances the impression.

———

▪ Place the silk fern at the top, along with some of the cornflowers.
▪ Add the wheat and bring the cornflowers down in the design to the outside.
▪ Insert the daisies at the centre.
▪ Fill in with plastic fern and ivy leaves.

SILK FLOWERS

MATERIALS Container. A variety of silk flowers – sweet peas, freesias, roses, lilies; silk fern, plus oddments of silk rose leaves.

Silk flowers are useful to make up a design well in advance of when you need it. I have used a group of silk summer flowers in this mauve and pink arrangement.

▌ Starting with two pieces of silk fern make a diagonal line, then add some shorter stems near the first placements to strengthen the outline.
▌ Add the lilies, bringing some nearer the front and flowing over the rim of the container.
▌ Add a few short pieces of silk rose leaves to help hide the front mechanics.
▌ Place the roses at the top and centre, and fill in with freesias, sweet peas and silk foliage to complete the arrangement.

Two more silk roses to bring a little more weight to the centre of the design would have improved it, but, alas, all the other colours in my box clashed!

SILK DAFFODILS

MATERIALS Cherub soap-dish, floral-foam pin, adhesive clay, small piece of floral foam. Silk daffodils, silk ivy leaves, dried moss.

This small arrangement is ideal for a dressing table or a coffee table.

▌ Stick the foam pin to the centre of the dish with a small amount of the adhesive clay, and place a small block of foam on the pin.
▌ Starting with the tallest flower, create a curving outline.
▌ Add a few ivy leaves at the back, then fill in with more flowers, keeping part of the cherub showing.
▌ Bring a few more flowers to the front, along with the ivy leaves.
▌ Add a little moss at the back to hide the foam.

CHRISTMAS TRIANGLE

MATERIALS Bronze cherub, ribbon loops. Various gold-plated leaves, handmade poinsettias, gold-painted fir cones.

Plastic leaves collected over a period of time are the main ingredients of this Christmas design. It has the advantage of being able to be made up in advance – very useful during the busy holiday season. You could add baubles or bells if desired.

▌ Insert the three long, spiky leaves and use the finest shapes on the outside to give the outline.
▌ Put in more leaves, concentrating the heaviest toward the centre, and add the gold-painted fir cones.
▌ Place the tallest and smallest poinsettias at the top, and bring the large one to the centre as a focal point.
▌ Add red ribbon loops to carry the colour through the design.

To make the poinsettias see page 16.

MODERN CHRISTMAS

MATERIALS White container, soaked floral foam, three baubles, red base. Three white-painted cane loops, carnations, spray carnations, holly, yew.

▌ Insert the three loops into the floral foam within the container, spacing them out with the largest at the back and the smallest to the front.
▌ Add a bauble to one side, and one in the centre.
▌ Add three large carnations and fill in with the spray carnations, bringing them forward.
▌ Add the holly and yew to fill in the gaps and hide the mechanics.
▌ Place the arrangement on the base.

This economical design is a modern arrangement, and makes a nice change for Christmas.

HALLOWEEN

MATERIALS Tin can containing pinholder with soaked floral foam in front, black base, witch, pumpkin. Black-painted wood, an assortment of glycerine-preserved material, chrysanthemums.

▌ Impale the wood on the pinholder at the back of the container.
▌ Add tall pieces of preserved material at the back, along with small chrysanthemums.
▌ Bring the heavier preserved pieces lower down in the arrangement, forming an asymmetrical line.
▌ Put in the heavy chrysanthemums and preserved leaves; fill in the gap with leaves and flowers.
▌ Place on the base.
▌ Add the witch to one side, and the pumpkin to the other.

The pumpkin is moulded from filler compound; when nearly dry it had a 'face' gouged out. The face was then painted black and the pumpkin orange.

EASTER DESIGN

MATERIALS Tin can with soaked floral foam, cane base, coloured packing straw, two chicks, eggs, Easter ribbon. Freesias, nephrolepsis fern, carnations, spray carnations.

▪ Use the freesias and fern for the outline.
▪ Add the buds of the spray carnations to the top, and those more open to the centre. Add large carnations to the centre.
▪ Add freesias, carnation spray and fern to fill in, bringing them well over the edge of the container.
▪ Place the arrangement on the base.
▪ Arrange the packing straw on the base with the chicks and eggs. Put the Easter ribbon around the outside of the base.

This design could have chocolate eggs or an Easter bunny as alternative accessories.

ST. PATRICK'S DAY ARRANGEMENT

MATERIALS Bowl, adhesive clay, pinholder, green base. Two dried stems of allium, *Helleborus corsica*, *Helleborus foetidus*, medium fatsia leaf.

This arrangement was made simply because I had two dried stems of allium which, when placed together, resembled a harp. I thought this would be ideal for the basis of a St. Patrick's Day arrangement.

▪ Put a little adhesive clay on the join of the stems, then place on the pinholder. Add some water to the bowl.
▪ On one side of the bowl goes the longest stem of the hellebore, followed by the shorter stems.
▪ Other short pieces of hellebore are placed at the front to cover the mechanics.
▪ Add the fatsia leaf to the opposite side.
▪ Place the arrangement on the green base.

The fatsia leaf is the 'hand' playing the harp. You could add a leprechaun or a cut-out shamrock as an accessory, if desired.

AN ARRANGEMENT FOR ST. VALENTINE'S DAY

MATERIALS Gold stand with small gold-sprayed tin can stuck on top, soaked floral foam, large heart, cherub, small hearts, Baccarat roses with leaves, spray carnations.

A romantic arrangement for lovers' day.

The large heart is cut from stiff cardboard and covered with ribbon. Cover the point first by glueing ribbon on, then winding it around until the heart is completely covered. Glue the ends. Wind a stiff wire around the base so that you can push it on to the floral foam.

The small hearts are red pipe-cleaners, wired at the ends with a stiff wire bound with gutta-percha or crepe paper and simply pushed into heart shapes.

▌ The large heart is added to the centre back of the floral foam.

▌ A long-stemmed rosebud is inserted on one side, and a shorter rose on the opposite side.

▌ Cut the roses and bring them down to the centre, with some of the flowers going behind the heart and others in front.

▌ The small cherub (a Christmas angel doubling as Cupid) is placed in front of the heart, and spray carnations are used to fill in the gaps.

▌ Rose leaves are added to back the flowers and to hide the mechanics.

▌ The arrangement is placed on a red velvet base.

The variation has the large heart removed and the small hearts placed so that they run through the design.

EDWARDIAN-STYLE BASKET

MATERIALS Basket, tin can with soaked floral foam. Spray carnations, gypsophila (baby's-breath), ferns, carnations.

The old-fashioned basket was the inspiration for this design. The Edwardians loved ferns, carnations and gypsophila. This arrangement is based on a picture in one of my old flower books. It would have contained a lot more fern and a huge ribbon bow tied to the handle, but I have made it a little more suitable for today's style of arranging.

▌ Start with the spray carnations at the top and make a diagonal line, leaving a good portion of the handle free.
▌ Add gypsophila and ferns, continuing the line.
▌ Add the heavier carnations running through the centre of the design, adding more of the spray carnations, gypsophila and ferns as you go to fill the gap.

If you should want to make it look more like a period design, add some fine buttonhole fern, and trail a piece around the handle. Put a large bow of matching ribbon low down on the bare side of the handle.

POSY DESIGN

MATERIALS Glass vase with candle cup on top filled with soaked floral foam and taped to the top, small base. Gypsophila (baby's breath), spray carnations, euonymus foliage.

This posy design made on a tall container could be used in a buffet decoration for a wedding.

▌ Cut the gypsophila into small pieces and make a round shape, taking it to the back and sides.
▌ Place the carnations all around, using buds as well as fully opened flowers.
▌ Fill in with euonymus.
▌ Place on the base.

This design could also be made in a small container, which would be suitable to place along the length of a bride's table. Colours could match the bridesmaids' dresses.

A suite at The Fairmont has always been considered the standard of luxury in business travel.

Indeed, there was a time when it was a luxury afforded to only the very few. Or, the Very Important. Like Presidents. Royalty. And even the occasional Pope.

President William H. Taft was one of many who enjoyed a suite at The Fairmont. Now, so can you.

on a complimentary or reduced rate basis.

As a President's Club member, you will also receive deluxe welcome gifts, as well as a special dining certificate and complimentary overnight shoeshine. In the morning, look forward to coffee or tea, and your choice of newspaper, delivered to your room.

It used to take money, power and influence to get a suite at the Fairmont. Now, it just takes a signature.

But today, you needn't be registered in Who's Who to open doors at The Fairmont. You simply need to register in our President's Club.

Every time you check into a Fairmont, you will automatically be upgraded to a suite,

when one is available, at no extra charge.

What's more, you'll enjoy guaranteed room availability whenever you make your reservations at least 48 hours in advance — even when a city is sold out. As well as access to our Health Clubs and Business Centers

But that's not all. Because if you belong to the American Airlines® AAdvantage® program, you'll earn 500 miles with every stay.

President's Club membership is completely free. To enroll, just call 1-800-522-3437.

No other hotel makes it so easy for guests to experience this level of elegance, comfort and style.

But then, at The Fairmont, we consider a Very Important Person and a guest to be one and the same.

THE Fairmont

AMERICA'S GRAND HOTELS. SINCE 1907

CHICAGO	DALLAS	NEW ORLEANS	SAN FRANCISCO	SAN JOSE/SILICON VALLEY
$165	$125	$119	$175	$125

was Cubans living in exile in Miami who bought the stuff. But recently, with the wave of interest in all Latin American art, collector interest in Cuban works is broadening. At the big auctions Cuban art is now second in volume only to Mexican art. Prices, naturally, have been rising. Cuban works now fetch $5,000 to $300,000.

It was not always thus. The Cernudas got into a big jam for collecting the old masters. In 1989 U.S. Customs agents raided the Cernudas' home and seized their entire art collection, claiming it violated the U.S. embargo with Cuba. After four months and $150,000 in legal fees, a federal judge ruled that the Cuban art was educational material, like film or literature, and protected by the First Amendment. The paintings, which still bear labels marked "Evidence," went back to the Cernudas.

"It was the catalyst that finally cleared the whole situation up," says

Clockwise from upper left: old master paintings by Mario Carreño, Angel Acosta León and Mariano Rodríguez.

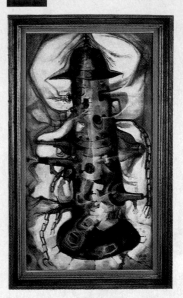

Photographs by Mark M. Lawrence

Ramón and Nercys Cernuda with "Eva," 1940 (left) and "Bandolero Cubano," 1943, by old master Carlos Enríquez
Castro is cashing in with forgeries.

Lisa Palmer, head of Christie's Latin American art department.

The ruling gave a big boost to work done by Wilfredo Lam and the other old masters. One Lam painting sold for $600,000 at Christie's in 1991.

Leave it to Castro. Now that all Cuban art is legal in the U.S., and can fetch six figures, Castro could well raise badly needed foreign exchange by selling the art he confiscated when he seized power. But that would be too bourgeois for Castro. Instead, he is exporting fakes. By the boatload.

Forgeries of both the old masters and other artists are now churned out in Cuba, exported to Spain and Mexico, or smuggled into the U.S. Wilfredo Lam forgeries have helped drive down prices for his bona fide art by about 20%. "For every authentic Lam, I see three or four fakes," says August Uribe, head of Sotheby's Latin American department.

To avoid getting taken by Castro and other crooks, stick to the leading galleries. Some of the best dealers include the Gutierrez Fine Arts, the Fred Snitzer Gallery and Elite Fine Art, all in Miami. In New York there are Sotheby's, Christie's, Nohra Haime Gallery and Frumkin/Adams. And in Mexico City, hunt out the Galería Nina Menocal.

For over 43 years, leading international companies have selected *VISION* to advertise their products, goods and services throughout Latin America.

- **Reaching Latin America's top business influences and consumer trendsetters**

- **Edited in Spanish by Latin Americans for Latin Americans**

- **ABC-Audited 180,000 circulation base**

- **75% fully paid subscribers providing readership continuity**

- **Full coverage of the 18 markets of the region as well as regional & single country advertising editions**

- **Lower effective CPMs than any international magazine circulating in the region**

- **Integrated marketing services and free translation**

- **24 issues per year**

From Miami to New York, Cuban art is hot, hot, hot.

Castro's last cache

By Christie Brown

WHEN IT CAME TO ART, Fidel Castro had a choice to make upon seizing control of Cuba in 1959: promote art as propaganda; or as a way to win cultural prestige and bring in badly needed foreign exchange.

Cachet—and cash—beat communism.

Before Castro there were Cuban artists who enjoyed international reputations, chief among them Wilfredo Lam (1902-82), Amelia Peláez (1897-1968), René Portocarrero (1912-86), Carlos Enríquez (1900-55) and Mariano Rodríguez (1912-90). These artists painted in modernist and surrealist styles.

Castro's government wound up owning many works by these Cuban "old masters," having seized them from the homes of wealthy Cuban exiles or acquired them directly from the artists.

For exportable art the Castroites turned to younger artists. They could paint whatever they wanted, and as much as they wanted (as long as there was no overt criticism of Castro). However, most works had no hard propaganda messages, unlike Russian art at the time. But in return for leaving the artists alone, and supplying them with materials, Castro would keep about 50% of whatever their art fetched from foreign buyers.

Obviously, not all Cuban artists were happy with this arrangement or with Castro's misrule. Many fled to the U.S. as soon as they could.

The first wave was the budding

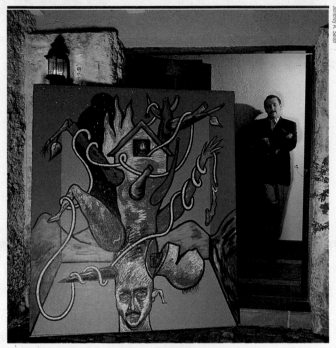

Fernando Alvarez-Perez with "Tree of Old Memories," by Sixties-generation artist Luis Cruz Azaceta
The elite artists Castro sponsored are also leaving in droves.
▬

"The Jungle," by Wilfredo Lam
For every real Lam, expect four fakes.
▬

artists who left Cuba in the 1960s and trained in the U.S. They were followed by a second group of painters, those who left during the Mariel boatlift in 1980.

The last to arrive here were Cuba's elite artists. Promoted and shown internationally under Castro, they have been defecting in droves over the last four years.

One major collector of living Cuban artists is Dr. Fernando Alvarez-Perez, an obstetrician in Coral Gables, Fla. While helping out with the arrival of Mariel refugees, he met some of the artists and got hooked. His collection includes about 100 works.

The paintings by the newest arrivals differ markedly in style from those of the earlier émigrés. While works by the Sixties generation and Mariel school artists show American influences, the works by recent Cuban defectors have a very international, avant-garde style.

Although many of these Cuban artists now paint side by side in Miami, there is no love lost among the three groups. Each believes the others had it easier than they did. Yet for all their stylistic and political differences, their paintings all have a common theme: anger and rootlessness.

However, there is also much that is essentially Cuban about a good deal of the art. Cuban exiles Ramón and Nercys Cernuda of Miami have amassed over 300 of the so-called old master paintings. For the Cernudas the paintings depict the soul of their homeland, blending Spanish, African and Chinese cultures. Pointing to a 1946 modernist painting of a rooster by Mariano Rodríguez, they race each other to describe it. "The rooster symbolizes machismo culture—very rebellious, very dignified," says Ramón. "Colorful," adds Nercys. "Sensual, promiscuous," says Ramón. "Loud," says Nercys. Ramón laughs, "It's a very Cuban animal."

Very Cuban and very in. At first i

The surprise of wisteria? How perfectly it moves indoors. The lavender color looks fresh and new; the vine motif lends itself to charming stencil traceries.

● Inviting wisteria to take over a room may be the prettiest idea to come along in ages—the secret is to tone your decorating to the grace and delicacy of the flower. Keep your color scheme pale, furniture simple, the whole mood light and airy. An easy way to start off: use wisteria-patterned sheets. This sumptuous table is layered with *two*—a twin-size (trimmed with grosgrain) for the square cloth, king for the round, and both are a breeze to make. Contrast with solid lavender cushions on chairs and tie-on arm rests to match. The drapes? Sheets again. Use one twin or full-size for each panel; sew a casing across top. To carry on the wisteria motif, stencil flowery vines around windows and a mirror frame (trail a tendril or two on mirror itself!). Stencil some napkins too; then slip into rings of *faux* wisteria you twine and hot-glue in a circle.

Photos: wisteria, Margaret Hensel/ Positive Image; all others, Jeff McNamara. Curtain and tablecloth fabrics from Springmaid. Chairs, the Door Store. Wall-covering, Bob Mitchell Designs. Terra-cotta tiles, Country Floors. Rug, ABC Carpet and Home.

There are dozens of ways (besides a bowl of American Beauties!) to fill your home with roses. Cut them, stitch them, glue them, drape them—for an intimate world of blooms.

● For a room that's coming up roses, think pink—all shades of pink, in stripes and plaids, prints large and small—to set your backdrop. Add green and cream, then scatter roses everywhere! You might begin by stitching a round rose cushion for a chair back, dressing windows in the same rose fabric, *opposite.* Or decorate a spectacular mirror by painting the frame a deep green, then covering it with papercut-outs—simple *decoupage.* The candle shades? They're store-boughts you embellish with tiny garlands applied with hot glue. Pillow talk *(above)* sends more flowery messages. You make the rose-strewn beauty (on sofa) with a napkin and fringe; the candy-striped kitty is simple stitch-and-stuff. As for the needlepoint design (on chair), it's an FC kit you trim as you like (order yours, page 122). Another blooming touch: A trio of botanicals hung from huge bows. (Order the prints, page 122.) For the pretty plate, *right*—mount wrapping-paper roses on *the back* of a glass dish with white glue, spray-paint.

Photos by Jeff McNamara. All fabrics (Trevira/cotton blend) from Stevens. Accessories from Fitz & Floyd, Charlotte Moss & Co., The Three Weavers and Stelton U.S.A. Inc. Decoupage mirror and plate designed by Dale Joe and Jack Champlin. For more information, see Buyer's Guide, page 106.

FAMILY CIRCLE'S
HOW TO!
see page 118

# of Flowers

No need to sit on a garden bench to drink in the beauty of a tumble of roses—or any other bloom! You can bring the glory of flowers *indoors* with our decorating ideas. Pick from rose, wisteria or sunflower themes and discover the prettiest projects ever, like a decoupage mirror and a striking floorcloth. You'll also find almost-instant spruce-ups (lampshades, for example) plus ingenious touches that turn a whole room flowery. Bloom bonus: how to start a rose garden, see page 116.

Photos: *(left)* © Christopher Baker, from *The Glory of Roses*, by Allen Lacy, published by Stewart, Tabori & Chang; *(right)* Wayside Gardens.

TABLE DECORATION

MATERIALS Covered tin can with soaked floral foam, candle holder, candle, cake stand. Michaelmas daisies, chrysanthemums, *Alchemilla mollis*.

▌ Place the candle holder in the middle of the floral foam.
▌ Insert the cut stems of the Michaelmas daisies to form a low outline.
▌ Add chrysanthemums with buds on the outside, the heavier flowers toward the centre.
▌ Add more Michaelmas daisies, cutting them short and inserting them between the chrysanthemums.
▌ Fill in the gaps with *Alchemilla mollis*.
▌ Place on the cake stand and insert the candle into the holder.

This design can be made without the candle; just replace the candle and holder with a flower in the centre, keeping it low in the design.

THREE-TIER ARRANGEMENT

MATERIALS Three-tier container, soaked floral foam. Chrysanthemums, cupressus (cypress).

This design is useful for a buffet arrangement, since it's easy to make and it doesn't take up much space.

▌ Cut the floral foam into small blocks to fit around the central column of the container.
▌ Put in the chrysanthemums, cut short, around the three tiers.
▌ Add cupressus to hide the mechanics and to fill in the spaces between the flowers.

PEW END

BRIDESMAID'S POSY

MATERIALS Soaked floral foam in container with handle, taped for security; ribbon loop and ribbon tail, wire. Cupressus (cypress), privet, spray carnations.

MATERIALS Soaked floral foam, posy holder, posy frill, narrow ribbon for handle, wider ribbon for loops and tail, thin wire, stub wire, gutta-percha. Ivy leaves, roses, spray carnations.

▌ Make a framework all around the container with the cupressus, making it longer at the end opposite the handle.
▌ Add the privet in between.
▌ Insert the buds of long flowers at the end opposite the handle, and, cutting the carnations fairly short, fill in with them at the side and centre.
▌ Add the ribbon loops and fill in the gaps with the privet.
▌ Fold the ribbon tail nearly in half, and twist a stub wire around the fold; then push at the back into the foam.
▌ Cut the ends into a 'V' shape to finish.

▌ Push the posy frill on to the handle of the holder until it reaches the top.
▌ Bind the handle with the narrow ribbon, and twist a small piece of thin wire tightly around the top to secure the ribbon. Tie on the tail over the wire.
▌ Place small ivy leaves around the rim of the holder with wired loops finished with gutta.
▌ Add a rose at the centre, and place four more lower down at equal distances around it.
▌ Add the carnations in between the roses and near the base of the holder.
▌ Fill in the gaps with more carnations and rose leaves.

If making these for a flower festival when a budget has to be adhered to, use only foliage, making sure you have plenty of yellow leaves and a few ribbons of contrasting colour. These will look most effective in spite of having no flowers.

This arrangement can also look attractive when made with dried or silk flowers.

ARRANGEMENT IN A SHELL

MATERIALS Shell containing soaked floral foam. Heuchera, lily-of-the-valley leaves, *Alchemilla mollis* leaves, spray carnations.

Shells make lovely containers, and although this one doesn't hold a great deal of foam, it still sustains an attractive arrangement.

▌ Fill the shell with the soaked foam.
▌ Make an outline of heuchera, bringing some over the front.
▌ Add the leaves, following the line.
▌ Insert the carnations to finish the arrangement.

HORIZONTAL DESIGN

MATERIALS Painted tin can filled with soaked floral foam, oval base. Roses, spray carnations, *Alchemilla mollis*.

- Begin with the rosebuds to form a low outline.
- Add the carnations and *Alchemilla mollis*.
- Bring the fuller flowers toward the centre.
- Fill in the gaps with alchemilla and its foliage, along with a few more leaves.
- Place on the base.

This small design is suitable for the top of a bookcase or a coffee table. It could also be used as a table decoration.

THE DANCER

MATERIALS Figurine container filled with soaked floral foam. Weigela, spray carnations, roses.

- Insert the weigela to form an arch over the figurine.
- Add the spray carnations to the sides.
- Place the roses so that they are running through the design.
- Fill in with spray carnations, rose leaves and short pieces of weigela to hide the mechanics.

Any garden flowers, such as sweet peas or side shoots of larkspur, would look attractive in this type of arrangement.

SIMPLE IRIS ARRANGEMENT

MATERIALS Narrow pot, filled with soaked floral foam, tile base. Five irises, four ivy leaves.

▌ Insert an iris bud at the top, and two more lower down, on slightly different levels.
▌ Add the last two irises with the lowest one coming over the rim of the container.
▌ Back this with ivy leaves, which will hide the mechanics.

This design is an easy one for a beginner to tackle. Any medium-sized leaves could be used for the backing.

CREAM AND WHITE

MATERIALS Cherub container filled with soaked floral foam. Bride gladioli, lilies, acuba foliage, fern.

▌ Insert the bride gladioli to give a slightly curving asymmetrical line.
▌ Add the lilies, with the opened ones at the middle of the design.
▌ Use acuba and fern to create a framework for the centre lily, and fill in any remaining gaps with ferns.

PETITE SHELL ARRANGEMENT

MATERIALS Shell container, soaked floral foam. Dried flowers of dyed sea lavender, xeranthemum, statice, tansy, santolina; hare's-tail grass.

This is a 'petite' arrangement, which is defined as one under 9in (23cm) in size. The shell container was picked up on the beach and glued to another shell for use as a base.

■ Insert the sea lavender to give a curving outline.
■ Add the xeranthemums to the outside and over the rim.
■ Add the statice, tansy and santolina to the centre.
■ Fill in with a few hare's-tails and a little more sea lavender.

PETITE SHOE

MATERIALS Shoe filled with soaked floral foam. *Lonicera nitida*, heuchera, feverfew, aubretia, *Alchemilla mollis*.

■ Make a slightly curving outline with the lonicera.
■ Add the heuchera to follow the line.
■ Place the feverfew through the design, with slightly larger flowers at the centre.
■ Put in aubretia, alchemilla and a few more stems of lonicera to fill in any gaps.

This little arrangement conforms to the definition of a 'petite' design, i.e., under 9in (23cm), so be sure to use flowers to scale.

SEA SHELLS

KITCHEN GARDEN ARRANGEMENT

MATERIALS Stick in bottle held in place with modelling clay, blue drape, fishing net, large bulldog clip, tin can with soaked floral foam, two abalone shells. Bride gladioli, irises, spoon chrysanthemums, *Ballotta pseudodictamnus, Senecio greyii*, anemones.

This design is an exercise to try and bring out the colours of the pearly abalone shells, which are pink, mauve, white and blue.

▌ Place the blue drape over the stick and put the fishing net over the top, securing it at the back with the bulldog clip.
▌ Spread the drape to form an approximate asymmetrical line.
▌ Starting with the tallest flower, follow the line of the drape, using the gladioli, irises and chrysanthemums.
▌ Insert the ballotta and senecio to one side.
▌ Place more flowers at the base, bringing some of them forward.
▌ To complete the design, add one shell at the back on one side, and one nearer the front on the opposite side.

MATERIALS Pheasant feathers, stone jar, small jug, soaked floral foam, cocktail and kebab sticks, wood base, fresh or plastic grapes. Flowers of sage and chive, fennel, onions, apples, mint, celery, lemon balm, parsley, lemons.

This arrangement utilizes plant material from your garden and your fruit bowl. It is suitable for a kitchen arrangement – and you can always eat it when you are tired of the arrangement!

▌ Make a framework of the pheasant feathers, and strengthen the outline with the sage and fennel.
▌ Add the chives to the top and sides.
▌ Add the onions impaled on kebab sticks.
▌ Insert a few apples on cocktail sticks in the middle.
▌ Fill in the gaps with the mint, celery, lemon balm and parsley.
▌ Place the design on the base.
▌ Group the apples and lemons at the base, and use the grapes to follow the line.
▌ Add the jug to the opposite side with a small bunch of grapes behind it to complete the design.

ORCHIDS WITH A FIGURINE

MATERIALS Base, tin can, pinholder with soaked floral foam in front, figurine. Wooden loops, ivy leaves, wisteria-vine ferns, Singapore orchids, apples, grapes, cymbidium orchids.

This arrangement has a tropical feel to it because of the association of the plant material and figurine to tropical countries.

▌ Place the tin can on the base.
▌ Impale the wood on the pinholder at the back.
▌ Add the ivy leaves at the front, and the iris leaves and ferns along with a few Singapore orchids on one side.
▌ Add apples and grapes on the base.
▌ Add cymbidium orchids.
▌ Place the figurine in position on the base.

Any tropical-plant material of similar size and shape could be used for this design.

MINIATURE DESIGN

MATERIALS *First arrangement* – brown container with soaked floral foam, heuchera side shoots, flowers of santolina, small piece of cupressus (cypress). *Second arrangement* – jug with soaked floral foam, side shoots of heuchera, aubretia, leaves of rue *(Ruta graveolens)*, London pride, *Lonicera nitida*.

———

These tiny arrangements are termed 'miniature', which is defined as any design under 4in (10cm). It is fun to do either just one or a whole collection; even finding tiny containers can be enjoyable, and a collection can soon be amassed.

———

■ *First arrangement:* Insert the santolina flowers along with side pieces of heuchera, then carefully place a few very small pieces of cupressus to fill in and cover the mechanics.
■ *Second arrangement:* Insert tiny pieces of lonicera to form the outline, then insert small pieces of coral heuchera. Add aubretia along with the London pride. Bring the rue over the rim of the container, and tuck tiny pieces of lonicera into the back to hide the mechanics.

'LAST NIGHT AT THE PROMS'

MATERIALS Painted tin can with soaked floral foam, large base, party streamer, sheet music. Cane leaves, black-painted trimmed palm leaves, carnations and spray carnations, iris leaves, magnolia leaves.

———

This is an interpretive design to portray the traditional final night of London's famous Promenade Concerts. The black canes are notched to represent flutes, black and white represent the piano and the orchestra, and the carnation is for the conductor's buttonhole. Party streamers are what the audience throw, and the music is 'Land of Hope and Glory', always sung on the last night.

———

■ Place the cane and palm leaves at the back and sides.
■ Add one palm leaf to the front.
■ Add buds and spray carnations at the side, bringing the large ones to the centre.
■ Fill in with the iris and magnolia leaves.
■ Add the party streamer to run through the design.
■ Place the design on a base and add the sheet music.

IN SEPIA

MATERIALS Marble container, two photos in re-production frames, two photos without frames, brown base, cream lace drape, stick in bottle, modelling clay, soaked floral foam in candle cup placed on top of marble container. Glycerined plant material including dock, foxglove seedheads, beech, laurel, yew, eucalyptus, *Grevillea robusta*; dried flowers of statice, helichrysum, gypsophila (baby's-breath); a few skeletonized magnolia leaves; hare's-tail and pampas grasses.

■ Insert dock, hare's-tail and pampas to give a triangular outline.
■ Add foxglove seedheads, statice and helichrysum.
■ Add a few more hare's-tails lower down.
■ Place skeletonized magnolia, beech and laurel near the middle, along with a few more flowers.
■ Fill in the gaps with small pieces of eucalyptus, grevillea and gypsophila.
■ Arrange laurel leaves so that they flow over the rim with the magnolias and pampas.
■ Place on the base, which has been positioned on the cream lace drape. The material is help up at the back by a stick secured in a bottle with modelling clay. Add the photographs to complete the design.

NATURAL LANDSCAPE

MATERIALS Small tin can with soaked floral foam, wood slice, china deer. Lime, oxeye daisies (*Chrysanthemum leucanthemum*), cow parsley (*Anthriscus sylvestris*, or Queen Anne's lace), oak foliage, ragwort (*Senecio squalidus*).

■ Starting with the stripped lime, place it at the back in the soaked foam, and use a small piece of wood to partially cover the container.
■ Bring a further piece of lime to flow over the rim of the container on the opposite side.
■ Add the daisies to run through the design along with the cow parsley, gradually bringing it to the front, together with a piece of the red-tipped oak foliage in between the flowers.
■ Use more oak to flow over the rim of the container, and add a few stems of ragwort near the middle to add a little contrast.
■ Place the finished arrangement on a wooden slab, and add the china deer to complete the picture.

Any wild material of similar shape could be used for this design, and appropriate alternative accessories could be a china squirrel, chipmunk or fox.

GLADIOLI WITH CORK RING

MATERIALS Three-opening container, tile on fabric-covered base, three cork rings, soaked floral foam. Gladioli and their leaves.

I wanted to explore the possibility of using a piece of cork I had. I cut it with a hacksaw, joining two of the resultant pieces together with extra-long pins to give an interesting design unit.

▌ Cut the three gladioli to different lengths with the most opened stem of flowers cut short. Place this flower in the lowest opening. Place the other flowers in the two other openings, adding a leaf and one looped leaf in the second opening.
▌ Loop a leaf in the lower opening with the most opened flower, together with another leaf.
▌ Stand on the base, then place the joined cork in front, and the single piece at the back.

The close-up shows the way the cork is pinned before the pins are finally pressed down.

DISCO

MATERIALS Black tin can filled with soaked floral foam, base (12in LP), two 7in records. Dried painted hollow stems, liatris, gerberas, large ivy leaves, thin cane, dyed hare's-tail grass.

▌ Place the tin can on the centre of the large record.
▌ Place the painted stems at the back and sides, and bring a short one to the front.
▌ Add the liatris, following the outline.
▌ Insert the gerberas in an irregular pattern, coming through the centre and sides, with one low down in the centre.
▌ Add the ivy leaves to hide the mechanics.
▌ Place the thin cane in the top of the tallest hollow stem, and drape it around the design. Put the other end in the floral foam.
▌ Add small bunches of dyed hare's-tails in the tops of the hollow stems.
▌ Place one small record on one side of the base, the other wedged at the top between the two stems.

This arrangement would be suitable for a teenager's birthday party.

MARITIME MUSEUM

MATERIALS Painted 'sky' backboard, sandy base, fishnet drape, painted tin can with soaked floral foam, shells. Aquilegia (columbine), irises, bride gladioli, Michaelmas daisies, green chrysanthemums, *Ruta graviolens* (rue), seaweed, driftwood, muscari seed-heads, aquilegia seedheads.

This interpretive design contains flowers suggesting the sea in its many moods, with the blue, mauve, green, white and grey colours alluding to the depths of the ocean and the foam of its spray, and the seed-heads resembling sea creatures.

■ Drape the net over the backboard over to one side.
■ Place the tin can near the net.
■ Insert the tallest flower at the back, then bring the flowers in a casual manner to form an asymmetrical line, with a few heavier flowers toward the centre.
■ Add the driftwood to hide the container, and carry the line to the opposite side by the use of shells and seaweed.

WOOD CARVING

MATERIALS Tin can with dry floral foam, wood slice, elephant. Dried and preserved material, including poinciana pods, coconut spathes, proteas, tulip seed-heads, eucalyptus, cones, beech leaves.

___

This is a design interpreting wood-carving. The wood-like structure of the various pods helps to further the theme, and the different shades of brown are the varying colours of woods. The elephant is of course the finished carving.

___

▋ Insert a large poinciana pod and coconut spathe at the back.
▋ Add proteas and tulip pods, and bring other material to form a slightly curving outline.
▋ Fill in with the heavy plant material at the centre, and a few preserved leaves to fill in the gaps.
▋ Place to one side on the wooden slab, and add the elephant.

___

You could add wood-carving tools or shavings as accessories.

'MACBETH'

MATERIALS Large painted tin can with soaked floral foam, two black teardrop-shaped bases, brown velvet drape, toy dagger, tartan drape. Thorns of *Rosa sericea pterocantha*, red roses, *Mahonia japonica* leaves, heather foliage, perennial cornflowers (*Centurea montana*).

___

Here plant material is used to portray the Shakespearean theme. The thorn roses and prickly mahonia are blood and battle; the heather foliage and thistlelike stems of cornflower, along with the tartan drape, represent Scotland. The two bases are the steps leading to the bed-chamber in which the murder was committed, and the dagger is the instrument of death.

___

▋ The thorns are stripped of their leaves to show better colour, and placed at the back of the arrangement.
▋ Place the tallest rose in the centre back, and gradually bring the roses down through the design, adding a few thorns between them.
▋ Add the mahonia leaves, and at one side the perennial cornflowers, with the heather foliage.
▋ Add a few more roses to fill in the gaps and to hide the mechanics.

'LA CAGE AUX FOLLES'

MATERIALS Wig stand, soaked floral foam, peacock feathers, base, scarf. Delphiniums, alstroemeria, carnations, spray carnations, gerberas, acuba foliage.

I love musicals, and my favourite of all time is 'La Cage aux Folles'. This arrangement is my tribute to the wonderful costume designs by Theoni Aldredge. This would make a fun arrangement for a party.

I gave the wig stand a little 'brain surgery' by gouging out the top of its head with a sharp knife in order to leave a space for a good piece of foam. This should be lined with kitchen foil to prevent leakage.

▌ Make an outline of peacock feathers, then add the delphiniums and alstroemeria at the top and sides.
▌ Insert the carnations, spray carnations and gerberas to the centre and sides of the design.
▌ Add the acuba foliage to fill in the gaps.
▌ Stand the design on the base and tie the scarf into a bow.

Conclusion

In this book, I hope I have provided you with sufficient ideas for creating beautiful – and economical – flower arrangements. These suggestions are just to get you started, and I do hope you will take my advice and become a member of a flower club or horticultural society, as well as add wild-flower and gardening books to your list of 'required reading'.

Classes in flower arranging are often available at Adult Education Centres, so make enquiries in your area to find out just what is available.

Try to visit as many flower shows as you can and talk to the exhibitors. You will learn a lot from them.

Don't be afraid to enter a show; most flower arrangers are nice people, and you will usually find them willing to help newcomers.

If you hanker for an expensive container save up for it, or throw out subtle hints as your birthday or Christmas draws near.

Collect exotic material piece by piece; you will soon build up a good collection. Always be on the lookout for things you can dry or glycerine. These can be added to your boxes of useful plant material.

I hope all my readers will really enjoy their flower arranging and get some fun from it. Now that you have finished this book, don't just sit there – go forth and create!

Bibliography

These books are some of my favourites; in all, they cover a wide range of floral subjects, examining many different aspects of flower arranging.

AARONSON, MARION. *Flowers in the Modern Manner*, London 1981.

CLEMETS, JULIA. *Flower Arrangements in Stately Homes*, London 1966.

COE, STELLA. *Ikebana*, London 1984.

CONWAY, GREGORY. *Conway's Encyclopaedia of Flower Arrangement*, New York 1957.

CYPHERS, EMMA. *Holiday Flower Arrangements*, revised, New York 1954.

DERBYSHIRE, JANE. *The Flower Arranger's Year*, London 1981.

FOSTER, MAUREEN. *Miniature Preserved Flower Arrangements*, London 1985.

KNIGHT, MARY G. *Abstract and Not So Abstract*, New York 1965.

QUIN, EARLEY LEE. *Japanese Free-style Arrangement*, New York 1964.

ROCKWELL, F. F. AND GRAYSON, ESTHER C. *Flower Arrangements in Color*. U.S.A. 1940.

SOUTAR, MERELLE. *The Driftwood Flower Arranging Book*, London 1967.

SPRY, CONSTANCE. *Favourite Flowers*, London 1959.

TAYLOR, JEAN. *Church Flowers Month by Month*, Oxford 1979.

VAGG, DAPHNE. *Flowers for the Table*, London 1983.

WILSON, ADELAIDE B. *Color in Flower Arrangement*, New York 1954.

INDEX

'A One-Flower Arrangement', 70
accessories, 14–15, *15*, 32
   choosing, 13
achillea (yarrow), 26, 63, 80
   dried, 22
Achillea filipendulina (Coronation Gold), 21
acuba foliage, 42, 64, 76, 77, 81, 83, 96, 107
agapanthus, 83
'Agapanthus' (arrangement), 83
Alchemilla mollis (Lady's mantle) 21, 38, 46, 50, 51, 91, 93, 94, 97
alder
   – cone stems, 32
   twigs, 59
'All-Foliage Arrangement', 64
'All-Green Arrangement', 46
allium, 81, 85
alstroemeria, *31*, 48, 51, 55, 58, 107
'Alstroemeria And Roses' (arrangement), 51
'An Arrangement for St Valentine's Day', 89
anemone, 19, 28, 98
Anthriscus sylvestris, 21, 72, 102
anthurium, *29*, 37, 82
'Anthuriums' (arrangement), 82
antirrhinum, *20*, 23
apples, 98, 99
aquilegia (columbine), 38, 43, 63, 64
'Arrangement On A Bottle', 55
'Arrangement In A Shell', 93
arrangements, *see under* separate titles
artificial flowers, 15, 17
arum lily, *20*
   wild, 22
aspidistra, 24
aubretia, 97, 100
'Autumn And Orangeade' (arrangement), 62
'Autumn Concerto' (arrangement), 67

Baby's breath (gypsophilia), 90, 102
background material, 14
Ballotta pseudodictamnus, 98
bases, 13–14
beech, 27, 46, 80, 102
   copper, 23, 53
   leaves, 106
Begonia rex, 24
bellflower (campanula), 63
berberis, 66
berries, 23
   hawthorn, 22
   rosehip, 22
'Berries and Roses' (arrangement), 50
bindweed, 22
bird of paradise (strelitzia), 23, *23*
'Black and Orange' (arrangement), 79
bleached wood, 56
'Blue and White' (arrangement), 68
books, recommended, for collecting, 35
bouquet, bridal, *33*
bride gladioli, 43
'Bridesmaid's Posy' (arrangement), 92
broom, 39
   Scotch, 43
   Spanish (*Spartium junceum*), 40, 45, 52
bulbs, 25
bulrushes, 77
buttercups, 41

camellia, 14
campanula (bellflower), 63
'Cane Loop With Carnations' (arrangement), 79
candytuft, 20
carnations, 19, 44, 48, 57, 76, 79, 87, 88, 90, 100, 107
   spray *31*, 44, 48, 53, 55, 58, 67, 87, 88, 89, 90, 92, 93, 94, 100, 107
'Carnation With Fasciated Wood' (arrangement), 76
celery, 98
Centurea montana, 106
chaenomeles (flowering quince), 39
charlock (*Sinapsis arvensis*), 72
Chincherinchee, 23
Chinese lanterns, 22, 26, 30
chive, 98
choisya, 46
'Christmas Triangle' (arrangement), 86
chrysanthemum, 19, 21, *31*, 38, 41, 45, 46, 47
   green, 105
   spoon, 98
Chrysanthemum leucanthemum, 22, 71, 72, 102
'Chrysanthemum, Wood And Bulrushes' (arrangement), 77
Cissus antarctica, 24
clover (*Trifolium pratense*), 71, 72
coconut spathes, 106
coleus, 24
colour, use of, 30–31
   schemes, *30*, 31
   wheel, 30–31
cones, 106
   alder, stems, 32
   fir, gold plated, 86
containers, choice of 10, 12, *12*, 13, *13*, 32
   basket, 13, 40, 90
   bottle, 10, 52, 53, 54, 58, 64, 98
   bowl, 12, 48, 70, 81, 82, 85
   box, 13, 38
   brass, 22
   candle cup, 10, 63
   candlestick, 10, 55, 58, 67
   ceramic, 41
   cherub, 13, 44, 46, 47, 51, 64, 85, 86, 96
   dish, kidney shaped, 65
   dolphin, 45
   figurine, 13, 94
   homemade, 70, 79
   jar, 43, 80, 98
   jug, 10, *31*, 39
   marble, 13, 102
   modern, 41
   plastic, 13, 24
   pot, 52, 57, 59, 98
   pottery, 22, 76
   shell, 12, 93, 97
   shoe, 97
   tall, 12, 83
   tankard, 45
   tin can, 50, 60, 61, 62, 63, 65, 67, 68, 69, 72, 74, 75, 76, 87, 88, 89, 91, 94, 99, 100, 102, 104, 105, 106
   three-opening, 47
   three-tier, 91, 103
   tub, 60, 72
   two-opening, 44, 56
   vase, 13, *13*, *25*, 29, 42, 48, 59, 90
   wooden, 13, 62, 71
   wrought iron, 66
convolvulus (bindweed), 22
copper beech, 23, 53
   leaves, 106
cork, 103
cornflowers, 43, 55, 64
   perennial (*Centurea montana*), 106
   pink, 48
   silk, 84

Coronation Gold, 21
corsage, 70
cow parsley (*Anthriscus sylvestris*) 21, 72, 102
cowslip, *21*
'Cream and White' (arrangement), 96
cupressus (cypress), 46, 55, 57, 61, 63, 64, 66, 91, 92, 100
currant, flowering, 28
'Curved Arrangement in Figurine', 63
cyclamen, 25
cymbidium (orchid), 65
cypress, *see* cupresses

daffodil, *18*, 19, 21, 22, 28
   silk, 85
dahlia, 19
daisy, Michaelmas, 91, 105
   oxeye (*Chrysanthemum leucanthemum*), 22, 71, 72, 102
   silk, 84
delphinium, 42, 68, 107
design, principles of, 28–9
   interpretive, 31–2
   one flower, 32
   special occasion, for, 32–3
   themes, ideas for, 31–2, 33
Dicenta formosa, 64
Digitalis purpurea, 22, 80
'Disco' (arrangement), 104
dock, 71, 80, 102
   seedheads, 46
'Down By The Riverside' (arrangement), 71
'Dress Up A Potted Plant' (arrangement), 78
'Dried Design' (arrangement), 80
dried flowers, *see* flowers, dried
'Driftwood With Chrysanthemums', (arrangement), 75
Dryopteris filix-mas, 80

'Easter Design' (arrangement), 88
'Eastern Influence' (arrangement), 60
echinops, 80
'Edwardian-style Basket' (arrangement), 90
escallonia, 53
equipment, basic, 10, *11*
   special, *11*
eucalyptus, 80, 102, 106
   dried, 106
euonymus, 48, 66
   foliage, 90
Euonymus japonica, 67
exhibiting, 35

fatsia leaf, 24, 44, 77, 88
ferns, 20, 62, 72, 84, 90, 96
   hart's tongue, 24
   maidenhair, 24
   male (*dryopteris filix-mas*), 80
   nephrolepsis, 74, 88
   plastic, 84
   silk, 84, 85
   wisteria-vine, 99
fennel, 98

'Ferns And Foxgloves' (arrangement), 80
feverfew, 97
figurine, 14, *14*, 32
fir cones, gold plated, 86
'Five Carnations' (arrangement), 44
flags (*Iris pseudacorus*), 71
flower clubs, 33–4, 108
   National Association of Flower Arranging Societies (NAFAS), 34–5
flower shows, exhibiting at, 35
   schedules, 34–5
flowering currant (Ribes genus), 28
flowers, artificial, 15, 17
   buying of, 17–18
   Christmas, 17, 86, 87
   dried, 22, 84, 92, 97, 102, 106
   Easter, 86
   festival, 92
   forcing, 27–8
   garden, 20–21, 48, 63, 64, 94
   growing habits, 19–20
   long-lasting, 22–3
   paper, 17
   plastic, 17
   seasonal, 18–19
   silk, 15, 84, 85, 92
   wild, 21–2, 72
'Flowers In A Candlestick' (arrangement), 58
foliage, 23–4, 24, 25–6, 66
   glycerinated, 23
   heather, 106
   oak, 102
   privet, 50
   skimmia, 39
   spring, 32
   yucca, 24
forget-me-nots, 39, 40, 55
forsythia, 27
foxgloves (*Digitalis purpurea*), 22, 80
   seedheads, 46, 80, 102
freesias, *28*, 58, 88
   silk, 85
'Fresh With Dried' (arrangement), 46

garden, kitchen, 98
geranium, 21
gerberas, 56, 75, 77, 104, 107
'Gerberas' (arrangement), 77
'Gerberas In Bent Container' (arrangement), 56
gladioli, 19, *20*, 70, 103
   bride, 43, 68, 96, 98, 105
'Gladioli With Cork Ring' (arrangement), 103
glass floats, 15
Gold heart (ivy), 20, 23
Goldenrod, 21
grapes, 99
grass, 23, 27, 71
   drying, 27
   hare's tail, 97
   pampas, 27, 102
'Green and White' (arrangement), 44
Grevillea robusta, 46, 80, 102
griselinia, 64, 76
gypsophila (baby's breath), 90, 102

'Halloween' (arrangement), 87
hare's tail grass, 97, 102, 104
hart's tongue fern, 24
'Hawaiian Memories' (arrangement), 65
hazel, 62
    catkins, 28
heather foliage, 106
hebe, 63
helichrysum, 22, 26, 102
Helleborus corsica, 88
    H. foetidus, 46, 88
heuchera, 53, 93, 97, 100
holly, 87
honesty (*Lunaria annua*), 20
honeysuckle, Japanese, 48, 63
'Horizontal Design' (arrangement), 94
hosta, 20
    leaves, 17, 50, 56, 58, 65, 71, 75, 79, 81
house plants, 24–5

'In A Box' (arrangement), 38
'In A Ginger Jar' (arrangement), 43
'In An English Garden' (arrangement), 63
'In Sepia' (arrangement), 102
indoor garden, 25
iris, 19, 20, 48, 62, 65, 96, 98, 105
    foliage, 81
    leaves, 41, 47, 56, 74, 81, 84, 100
    silk, 84, 85
'Iris And Fern' (arrangement), 62
Iris pseudacorus, 71
    I. siberica, 38
    I. unguicularis, 21
ivy, 25, 74, 85
    leaves, 43, 52, 60, 69, 70, 75, 81, 82, 92, 96, 99, 104
    'Gold Heart', 20, 23
    silk, 84

jacaranda pods, 65
Japonica eunonymus, 67
'Jug Arrangement', 39
'Just Buttercups' (arrangement), 41
'Just Three Alliums' (arrangement), 81

kalenchoe, 78
'Kitchen Garden Arrangement', 98

'La Cage Aux Folles' (arrangement), 107
Lady's mantle, 21, 38
'Lamp Accessory' (arrangement), 68
'Last Night At The Proms' (arrangement), 100
laurel, 46, 102
lavender, sea, dyed, 97
leaves, gold plated, 86
    plastic, 86
    yucca, 44
lemon, 98
    balm, 98
liatris, 18, 48, 104
lilac, 47, 48
lilies, 21, 52, 56, 64, 67, 76, 79, 96
    arum, 20
    kaffir (*Schizostylis cocconea*), 21
    silk, 85
    wild, 22
'Lilies And Contorted Hazel' (arrangement), 52
'Lilies And Wood' (arrangement), 76
'Lilies With Bleached Wood' (arrangement), 56
lily-of-the-valley, 21, 33, 65
    leaves, 93
lime, 102
'Lime And Blue' (arrangement), 42
linaria, 63
London pride, 100

long-lasting flowers, 22–3
lonicera, 66
Lonicera nitida, 97, 100
Lunaria, annua, 20
lupins, 59, 60
'Lupins In Blue Vase' (arrangement), 59
'Lupins In Wooden Container' (arrangement), 60

'Macbeth' (arrangement), 106
magnolia leaves, 57, 79, 81, 100, 102
Mahonia japonica (berries), 50, 80, 106
maidenhair fern, 24
marigolds, African, 21
'Maritime Museum' (arrangement), 105
'Mauve Mixture' (arrangement), 48
'Mauve Wood With Lilies' (arrangement), 69
Michaelmas daisies, 61, 91, 105
'Miniature Design' (arrangement), 100
mint, 98
mock orange (philadelphus), 60
'Modern Christmas' (arrangement), 87
'Modern Chrysanthemum Arrangement', 47
'Modern With Wood And Gerberas' (arrangement), 75
molucella, 80
moss, 32, 65, 77, 80
    dried, 85
muscari seedheads, 46, 50, 105

narcissus, 19
National Association of Flower Arranging Societies (NAFAS), 34–5
'Natural Landscape' (arrangement), 102
nephrolepsis ferns, 74
nerines, 21
nigella, 20

oak, 64, 72
    foliage, 102
'Odds And Ends' (arrangement), 67
'One Gladiolus' (arrangement), 70
onions, 98
'Open Crescent Arrangement', 45
orchids, 22, 74, 81
    cymbidium, 84, 99
    Singapore, 58, 65, 68, 84, 89
'Orchids, Fern And Willow' (arrangement), 84
'Orchids, Ferns And Figurines' (arrangement), 74
'Orchids With A Figurine' (arrangement), 99
'Orchids With Hostus' (arrangement), 81
oxeye daisies (*Chrysanthemum leucanthemum*), 22, 71, 72, 102

palm leaves, 79, 100
pampas grass, 27, 102
pansies, 40
parsley, 98
'Pastels' (arrangement), 55
peacock feathers, 107
pelargonium, 25
'Petite Shell' (arrangement), 97
'Petite Shoe' (arrangement), 97
'Pew End' (arrangement), 92
philadelphus (mock orange), 44
'Pink And Blue' (arrangement), 57
'Pink Flowers With Glass' (arrangement), 64
'Pink Mixture' (arrangement), 48
'Pink Monochromatic' (arrangement), 53

pinks, 63
plant material, 17–18, 23–4
    conditioning of, 25–6, 26
    drying, 26–7
    forcing, 27–8
    preserving, 26–7, 27
plantain, 80
    stalks, 44, 47
pods, dried, 65
    jacaranda, 65
    poinciana, 65, 106
poinsettia, 86
    artificial, to make, 16
pontilla, 63
poppy, 59
    seedheads, 57, 59
'Poppies' (arrangement), 58
'Posy Design' (arrangement), 90
potted plant (kalanchoe), 78
    dressing up, 25
primula, 25
privet, 23, 45, 64, 66, 68, 92
    foliage (*Ligustrum ovalifolium*), 50
    golden, 20
proteas, 100
pussy willow, 28

Queen Anne's lace, 21, 72, 102
'Queen Elizabeth' (arrangement), 21

ragwort (*Senecio squalidus*), 72, 102
rhus, 23
ribes genus, 28
Rosa sericea pterocantha, 106
    R. viridiflora, 21
rose, 19, 21, 43, 50, 51, 53, 61, 92, 94, 106
    baccarat, 89
    dog, 72
    leaves, 85
    red, 106
    silk, 85
    white, 33
rosebay willow herb, 21
rosehips, artificial, 67
'Roses And Wood' (arrangement), 62
'Roses With Figurine' (arrangement), 61
rue, 64, 66
Ruta graviolens, 23, 100, 105
sage, 38, 48, 98
'St Patrick's Day Arrangement', 88
Sanchus avensis, 72
sansevieria (mother-in-law's tongue), 24, 25
santolina, 97, 100
satin pod
saxifrage, 40
Scabious, 63, 64
Schizostylis coccinea, 21
'Sea Shells' (arrangement), 98
seaweed 105
seedheads, 22, 46
    dried, 26
Senecio greii, 55, 64, 98
'Silk Cornflowers' (arrangement), 84
'Silk Daffodils' (arrangement), 85
silk fern, 84, 85
'Silk Flowers' (arrangement), 85
silk flowers, 15, 84, 85, 92
'Simple Iris Arrangement', 96
Sinapsis arvensis, 72
Singapore orchids, 58, 65, 68, 84, 89
skimmia foliage, 39

sowthistle (*Sonchus avensis*), 72
Spartium junceum, 45, 52
spray carnations, *see* carnations
'Spring Basket' (arrangement), 40
'Spring Mixture' (arrangement), 47
Stachys lanata, 23
statice, 22, 97, 102
    dried, 97
stephanotis, 33
stitchwort, 22
stocks, 38, 48, 63, 64
stretlitzia (bird of paradise), 23, 23
streptocarpus, 25
'Swan Lake' (arrangement), 65
sweet peas, 63, 64
    silk, 85
sweet william, 48, 64

'Table Decoration' (arrangement), 91
tansy leaves, 72
    dried, 97
Tellima grandiflora, 44
'The Dancer' (arrangement), 94
themes, *see* arrangements
'Three Chrysanthemums' (arrangement), 41
'Three Tier Arrangement', 91
trees, small
    Garrya elliptica, 21
    pittosporum, 21
Trifolium pratense, 71, 72
tulip, 19, 21, 39, 40, 45, 47, 59, 60
    seedheads, 106
'Tulip In A Tankard' (arrangement), 45
'Tulips With Alder Cones' (arrangement), 59
twigs, alder, 59
'Two Tier Foliage Arrangement', 66
Typhus augustifolia, 65, 71

Vinca major, 22

'Walk In The Woods' (arrangement), 72
wallflowers, 39, 40, 47
weigela, 66, 94
wheat, dried, 55, 84
wig stand, 107
wild flowers, 21–2
'Wild Flowers And Wood' (arrangement), 71
'Wild Flowers In Wooden Tub' (arrangement), 72
willow, 57, 84
    contorted, 70
wood, 23, 62, 67, 77
    drift, 14, 23, 25, 32, 75, 76, 78, 105
    fasciated, 76
    painted, black, 77, 79, 87
'Wood Carving' (arrangement), 106

xeranthemum, dried, 97

yarrow, 21
'Yellow Monochromatic' (arrangement), 52
yew, 46, 87, 102
yucca, 14
    foliage, 24, 44